# GOD'S OPPORTUNITIES

The Rev. John A. Woolley was ordained a priest of the Church of England in 1964 and served parishes in the Diocese of Liverpool over the years 1963–1975. In that year he became Chaplain to the Ryhope Hospitals in Sunderland. Since 1983 he has been Chaplain to Hill End Hospital, St Albans.

Mr Woolley is the author of several books, including *I Am With You*, which is also published by Fount.

By the same author
available as a Fount Paperback

I AM WITH YOU

Other books by the same author

THE FRIENDSHIP OF JESUS
GETTING TO KNOW JESUS
HELLO, JESUS
5S AND 6S MEET JESUS

# GOD'S
# OPPORTUNITIES

## John Woolley

Collins
FOUNT PAPERBACKS

First published in Great Britain in 1986,
by Fount Paperbacks, London

Copyright © John Woolley 1986

Made and printed in Great Britain by
William Collins Sons & Co. Ltd, Glasgow

# Contents

Author's Preface 7

1. God Loves Interfering! 9

2. Such Variety! 19

3. The Light-Bringer 24

4. What Happened in Palestine? 32

5. God's Plain Intention 39

6. The Irresistible Combination 44

7. The Right Diagnosis 51

8. Nature Obeys 57

9. Embarrassing, But . . . 62

10. The Ultimate Challenge 68

11. Our Miracles Begin Here 73

12. "Mary!" 78

13. A Hard Act To Follow! 84

14. Why The Power Flowed 89

15. Wonders Have Never Ceased 94

16. Crisis-Encounters 99

17. Seeing God At Work 104

18. The Miracle-Name     113

19. Trust-Miracles     118

20. Letting-Go Miracles     124

21. Love-Awareness     132

22. Victory-Miracles     142

23. Darkness Shared     150

24. Miracles of Looking     156

25. Thank-You Miracles     162

26. Our Guest     169

27. Those Miracle-"Dates"     175

28. Miracle-Partners     182

29. Indispensable!     192

30. Dark World . . . Bright Road     199

# Author's Preface

It's always exciting to write about God at work . . . especially in areas where we used not to notice Him doing things!

We can read today of marvellous happenings, remarkable answers to prayer.

As if to balance this, there's a stronger than ever tendency to find "natural" explanations for the things which happen, and to say that God doesn't intervene in miraculous ways.

The anti-miracle point of view is that we shouldn't raise false hopes by encouraging people to expect miraculous answers to their problems.

While it is true that we ought not to lead people to "demand" miracles, it is also true that God constantly produces them!

Our book is about recognizing, and being thrilled by, God's interventions – both the spectacular and the quiet – in our lives.

Perhaps I should apologize, in advance, if some of the things dealt with are very familiar. By contrast, I should also apologize for those places where one or two of the suggestions seem, at present, to be a little out of reach! . . .

# 1

# God Loves Interfering!

The news for this universe is that we are not alone. When we take the trouble to look at the evidence, we find that God has been marvellously at work in a puzzling, impersonal-looking creation.

God has shown the most unlikely people how much He loves them; He has told the most unlikely people His plans!

&ast; &ast; &ast;

Let us admit straightaway that the setting which God has given Himself to work in can be grim. Much of what we see around us seems purposeless, and because of this, for every one who says, "Yes, God is there", there is someone else saying, "I'm afraid that it's all blind chance."

Many have eventually settled, of course, for a sad or cynical resignation about a creation which has such tremendous contrasts.

If I was to write endlessly about the miracle of life, about sunsets and cool mountain streams, about human achievements, and about people falling in love, it would seem, for many, completely inadequate – even hurtful. Those whose lives are, on the whole, dark places would say, with justification, "Well, if that's the miracle of life, it has certainly passed *me* by!"

A puzzling creation – which seems even worse, of course, when tragedy strikes – a loved one is found to have cancer, and a nightmare begins. God (if there is such a being) seems further away than ever. Yes, a God who can seem very hard to find. To be honest, even for "believers" there is so often an elusiveness about Him.

Because the natural processes, such as becoming ill and dying, appear just to work themselves out, many have also sadly concluded that God doesn't intervene in our heartbreak situations. But although God so often does not appear to step into certain processes of this "risky" world, I have found that He is, in fact, wonderfully active in countless situations resulting from some of these processes . . . including, for example, many of the sadder instances of premature bereavement, or of severe handicap.

We are aware, each day, of so much that can be shattering, but I am increasingly convinced that God *is* lovingly in control, and giving unique help where He sees that some of the consequences of the natural processes are hurting most. The idea that we have a sort of spectator God who doesn't go in for miraculous interventions, but is much more inclined to let His own laws work themselves out, proves to be a most faith-destructive idea.

Where there is this stoical miracles-don't-happen concept, I believe that God increasingly becomes an abstraction, and huge doubts about His very existence can come sweeping in.

One of the ways in which we become more sure of our "sometimes elusive" God is when we learn to *recognize* what He is doing. I don't necessarily mean just in the creative process (which can be a bit confusing), but in the details of each day, and in life's crises and challenges.

I know that there is a danger of "pretending" that God has been doing things, when it wasn't really Him at all. But there's a far greater danger . . . of failing to see the countless instances when He really is at work.

If we say that God is a God of love, then it's hard to believe that He just passively watches us. Everything about love suggests involvement and caring interventions.

## Recognition

According to which dictionary we consult (or which theologian we read) we'll find various definitions of a miracle. For the moment, perhaps we can see a miracle as a definite activity of the spiritual dimension within this material creation, which in some way changes the "natural" course of events. If a miracle is a breakthrough of this sort by God, then I'm sure that we are seeing miracles every day!

If we accept that there are these loving interventions and anticipations on our behalf, and begin to watch out for them, it won't be long before we actually see God's love (in which we "believe") actually being expressed.

We shall not devote whole chapters of this book to a few well-chosen and spectacular miracles (which always seem to happen to other people!) Instead, we shall concentrate on learning to *recognize* God (who is concerned with the smallest aspects of our lives) doing things for us . . . This is a recognition which becomes more and more thrilling and absorbing. At first God's activity will often be in ways known only to the individual concerned.

It's not a case of an impassive, "non-intervening" God at all! We could easily lose count, once we've learned to recognize God at work, of the opportunities which He takes in just one human life . . .

Without these very practical interventions, happening all the time, in which God lights up dark places, our world would be an even more daunting and "risky" place, and many could be forgiven for wanting to opt out. There are, in fact, so many interventions that they seem to merge into one big state of intervention . . . a permanent active and caring presence.

Sometimes people will criticize our "naïve" acceptance of God's miracle-work, and our expectation of miracles, but quite frankly, I think that anything less than this is a compromise faith . . . one in which God seems increasingly to become just an idea.

Life on this planet will usually include some experience of pain – physical or emotional. With many of us, both older and younger, those hurts may go very deep. Human compassion and human skill can partially help, but what we're really looking for is for God to interfere! We realize that only He can produce the drastic change needed.

Well, I'm sure that we can start looking forward to seeing more of that "interference", because this is a love-based creation, and God cannot possibly detach Himself from our needs. I believe that we can become really expectant, even if life has not been very kind so far.

Later in our book we'll think of some of the conditions *we* can make, which seem to encourage God's activity in our lives – although, of course, He doesn't have to work strictly according to the conditions we provide!

\*    \*    \*

There is another wonderful thing about starting to notice God at work. As we begin to recognize His influence upon circumstances, and His work *for* us, He is, in fact, doing things *in* us. Eventually, we discover that major personality changes, for example, have been happening in us. Recognizing God in the details has led to the later realization that some of the miracle-changes for which we have been longing have actually begun to happen. Or in other words, the little miracles (perhaps noticed only by ourselves), leading to the "larger" ones . . . which everyone can see.

The changes which God makes, especially for the expectant and observant person, are not superficial or merely subjective, but real and lasting.

Learning to recognize God providing for us and keeping so many potentially harmful things out of our lives, we find ourselves responding with a growing love and gratitude . . . two qualities which, in themselves, are miracle-producing.

And so . . . *we* see more and more examples of what God is doing . . . *He* sees His own work in us.

## New Viewpoint

I have found that once we've become expectant – ready to see, and feel grateful for, God's miracles – there seems to be no limit to what He can do for us. If only we will let ourselves believe that God has well and truly stepped into our situation, we find that He carries us along a kind of faith road . . . We discover that we have a faith which can start to detect the unseen dimension transforming the tangible one.

Recognizing God at work may be hard at first, but

when we are willing to accept that He is active because of His great concern for us, this recognition becomes increasingly natural. We acquire that new dimension, shared with God, to the way in which we see every-day happenings. God's opportunity-taking used to be completely undetectable, but now we start to realize the *sureness* of what He has been doing. And even when, for the moment, some of His work on our behalf cannot be detected, we find that instinctively we're now able to *thank* Him for that temporarily-undetected activity!

Without our escaping from the duties, the problems, and the hard facts of living, we find that God lets us live, partially, in a "heavenly" environment. As this spiritual environment becomes part of our every-day existence, we begin, even with our problems, to feel so sure of God that we don't envy others one bit!

It seems as though God just cannot give enough to one of His children who both recognizes, and appreciates, His caring interventions.

\* \* \*

One can quite understand non-believers when they say that "seeing God at work" is just self-deception, and that everything can be explained by the evolutionary process, and by natural cause-and-effect.

But believers!!! . . . Well, although there is much about creation we would still love to have explained, I'm sure that God wants "believers" to become quite expert in detecting the things He does. I believe that He wants us to see the things which He brings into our lives, all the unplanned and helpful contacts, all the things we're saved from, and not call them coincidences or "things which would have happened anyway".

God has shown us that He doesn't go in for skywriting or pressurizing, or brainwashing. Instead He gently, almost imperceptibly and in all sorts of ways, makes first one person, then another, aware of how much He loves them. This gentle influence, coming from a permanent presence with us, explains that instinct about God's love which so many people have, in spite of all the unpleasant "facts".

Wonderful opportunities for God are created by each waking up to our need, each prayer of even wanting to trust. These are responses to His gentle influence upon the human race, and it's as though He's saying to us, "You're becoming aware that you are loved . . . Now let Me start to *help* you."

That help, of course, is always an absolutely free gift, a love-gift . . . having nothing to do with our own "virtue" or otherwise!

Because of His love, and because of people's desperate needs, therefore, God (far from setting the system in motion and then sitting back) constantly intervenes in our affairs. . . .

After reading those inspiring books about certain miraculous events in some people's lives, many others can feel wistful and disappointed. They feel like saying, "Yes, I'm sure that God exists, and I'm pretty sure that He loves me, but I feel that He'll never do anything as spectacular as *that* for me."

I can sympathize, because I have felt that way. But wait a minute . . . Those inspiring incidents are just a tiny fraction of the vast range of the things which God does for people every day. His interventions are far, far more numerous than those spectacular miracles in books or articles.

\* \* \*

In the Bible, of course, we can read some rather amazing things, things which have made one or two religious "professionals" a little sceptical – especially in the late twentieth century. I think we shall find that we can believe those amazing things, that we can let ourselves be *thrilled* by them . . . remembering that God was making His presence unmistakably felt to people who just did not know where they were going.

God has so often used "signs and wonders" to convince people of His existence, some of them spectacular, some quiet and "private", but deep.

There were, of course, three breathtaking years in Palestine when Jesus came . . . God's opportunity-taking there for all to see. After a time, as we know, it became rather quieter, as the Church became increasingly "respectable", although countless individuals continued, quietly, to experience God's miraculous help.

Today we read of some wonderful acts of God. Is this because God has suddenly sprung into action? The more likely reason, I'm sure, is that we've started to recognize Him at work, after centuries in which most people stopped looking for miracles, or looking only for the very spectacular. At last we are starting to watch God pushing back the forces (both spiritual and material) which destroy human happiness.

## New Personalities!

I believe that in this universe God has given Himself a sort of opportunity potential. It's thrilling to see Him produce all sorts of contrasts in people's lives, as He takes those opportunities. These contrasts are not just in the physical realm, the one most associated with miracles, but also, of course, in the sphere of personality.

God is constantly helping . . .

> people full of fear or guilt to become radiant . . .
> tense people to become placid . . .
> pessimists to become eagerly expectant . . .
> wavering people to become strong believers . . .
> "apologetic" people to become bold . . .

He is constantly making changes in *us*, changes which automatically change our situations . . .

Yes, we have an *active* God, who all the time is doing things in response to our requests and to our simple trust. He is also doing them for some who may not be aware of Him, or even particularly interested in Him!

It is a good exercise for all of us who are "believers" quietly to ask ourselves, now and again, this logical progression:

> Do I *really* believe God is there?
> Do I *really* believe that He loves me?
> If so, do I believe that He just stands by, impassively?
> Or does He act – *frequently* . . . because of His love?

I am sure that God wants us to leave behind the old kind of vicious circle and become involved in a new kind of hopeful circle.

The **old** kind is:

> Expecting nothing . . . therefore experiencing nothing . . . therefore still expecting nothing.

The **new** kind is:

> Expecting . . . experiencing . . . and therefore expecting even more!

17

\*    \*    \*

I hope that those who feel, sadly, that miracles are not for them, will join us now on a journey. We are going to see God taking His opportunities, both past and present. I know we shall soon find that He hasn't forgotten us, and that we can expect Him, now, to reveal many more instances of His tremendous care for us.

Can we look at some familiar and not-so-familiar examples of God's miracles? Let us do it as part of learning, very shortly, to see things happening in our own lives.

# 2

# Such Variety!

The wonder of our existence (however long the process took!) is our obvious Miracle Number One. After that, there are quite a few more, of course . . .

There is the daily miracle of new life. A tiny baby, lovingly protected by its Mum, who God entrusts with this bundle of possibilities . . .

High on my list would be the wonder of God actually letting His children *see* Him . . . letting Himself become one of us! Our familiarity with the story of Jesus must not destroy for us what a crucial event it was, an event which changed the potential of each human being, whether they have realized it or not.

There is the miracle of mainly poor and uneducated men and women proclaiming God's secrets for at least three thousand years . . . just as if they had been having a fireside chat with Him. Those secrets are captured in an amazing collection of literature pointing to that wonderful happening – the arrival of Jesus. (Sorry to use the word "wonder" again, but how else could you describe it?)

There is the miracle of weak and often mixed-up people finding tremendous strength, which could come from nowhere else but God. Those very "limited" individuals discovering that they suddenly had eloquence, and courage, and power. We have only to think of the early Christians!

Then there are the miracles happening every day (especially, though not always, where someone has prayed):

> Sad situations marvellously changed . . .
>
> Faith unfolding like a flower in the lives of determined "non-believers" . . .
>
> Painfully shy people drawn out of themselves and greatly used by God . . .
>
> Peace found in circumstances where you'd expect to find exactly the opposite . . .
>
> Hospital beds the scene of dramatically-changed lives (we will be looking at some of these) . . .
>
> Faltering prayers bringing amazing, perfectly-timed results, where there had been no human ingenuity or intervention . . .
>
> Countless instances of God resolving a very difficult situation where all that has been done is to tell Him about it . . .
>
> Very sane, matter-of-fact people experiencing, during times of crisis, the strong sense of "Someone" uplifting them . . . so that they are never quite the same person again . . .
>
> All sorts of set-backs and disappointments made to serve a good purpose (often within minutes of being given to God).

Miracles, spectacular or quiet, happening every day, as God makes everything fit into a pattern for those who will trust Him.

## Blind Chance?

There is much to wonder at, and what we've just thought about represents quite a variety, doesn't it? Such contrasts, which you feel that only God could have brought about. There are so many of what I like to call God's shy miracles. It's only when you patiently find out what the situation was previously, that you realize something amazing has happened.

Although there is a voice insisting that the vast evolutionary process is just blind chance, we have only, for example, to think of someone of whom we are very fond, only to listen to a lovely piece of music, and something in us (something logical!) cries out, "It can't be pure accident." That is why some sceptical people, after a very moving life-experience, can catch themselves out thinking, "Perhaps it's not all blind chance?"

The list of things to wonder at can get quite long. In other words, it's as if there is an area of *light*, containing many marvellous things, in this mysterious universe. And so, what about the *dark* areas – where there is so much suffering, and God's work is far from obvious?

I feel that it is as though God is saying to us, "If you will begin to recognize, and be enthusiastic about, the more obvious wonders in My creation, I will start to show you some in the darkness as well."

This is one reason why we shall look at some of Jesus's spectacular miracles in what was, for so many, a very dark existence, and where life was cheap. I don't think we should see this as a three-year "fairy-tale" episode, contrasting with centuries of barren inactivity. It was more like a close and privileged look at work which God is doing all the time.

\*    \*    \*

I promise not to quote too many stories about amazing and instant cures, for that could leave many people feeling as far away from a miracle as ever! But there are remarkable things happening today – wonderful answers to prayer, wonderful interventions . . .

For example, while this book was being prepared, a young man in a sleepy old town in the south of England had the normal curvature restored to his eye, as people stood around and prayed for him.

A doctor whom I know was watching it all happen, and he was able to verify medically the "before" and "after". But there are quieter things, just as miraculous. At about the same time I saw the reconciliation, within seconds of a prayer being made, of two bitter enemies (details later). I also saw the transformation in a dear old man of nearly ninety, whose life had been made sheer hell through terrible feelings of guilt.

## Quiet, But Decisive

Yes, it's the *range* of God's work which is so important. It is as we recognize as God's interventions, those events which might at first seem to be mere chance that we gradually realize that miracles are normal, they are God "interfering" on our behalf each day.

The times when something which initially looks like a chance event but is later seen clearly as God's work, are numberless. And once we accept that a miracle is not always something to make a huge crowd gasp, we can stop apologizing, even slightly, for the countless "shy" (or gradual) miracles. Failing to appreciate the range of God's work and looking only for the occasional "spectacular" miracle means that so much has been missed.

Obviously it will take a little time for many people to have the right idea about miracles. God can still be seen as the head of a sort of "physical healing" cult, and He is judged by its results! Sadly, many lose their faith when looking only for the very dramatic. Thousands of miracles never make the headlines – for example, the experience of the miracle of joy in the most discouraging settings of illness and handicap. Often, these people have longed for the putting-right of some physical problem, and then found a wonderful sense of God's nearness and of His love for them. So strong has been the spiritual awareness, that even the healing of the physical problem has become secondary for them.

*     *     *

As we look at just how God has been breaking through into people's lives and read the experiences of some of those lives, I know that He'll be delighted! He'll be delighted that we have taken the trouble to notice Him taking His opportunities and He will remove many of our doubts in the process.

Wouldn't it be a great idea if we could have a completely new view of our life on this planet? The view of so many is that it is life lived in an austere-looking universe, into which the mysterious God intrudes from time to time (or indeed hardly ever).

Let's change that, shall we?

Those who are "believers" (strong or not-so-strong) can see their lives, even if often sad, as lived in the presence of a warm, loving, protective and very *active* God.

Into this cared-for world, perhaps thoughts of the cold puzzling universe will intrude . . . just occasionally!

# 3

# The Light-Bringer

One night, ever so quietly, came history's decisive miracle. As we know, the miracle occurred after a refugee race had, over a long period, had it knocked into their heads that God had plans for them!

The climax of those plans was Jesus – God seen in a human life, the spiritual dimension miraculously involved with the material dimension. Here, at last, was the architect of this universe, able to be seen, and able to talk with men and women about the mystery and the wonder of life.

There are, of course, people who cannot see it this way and we need to look at their views, but before we do, shall we see what this miracle event meant?

This decisive event was not that of a young Jewish idealist finding Himself more and more spiritually-gifted and then somehow "adopted" into the sphere of God (a popular view with some theologians). This was God's beloved Son, who had always been "part of" God. (I'll admit that the Godhead, or Trinity, isn't too easy to visualize!)

What was happening was that the Divine Son, the creative agent, was letting go of most of His "status" in order to identify, in a beautiful way, with the under-privileged and the misunderstood. The Divine Son, one with God, was becoming one with *us* as well! You cannot imagine a much greater involvement in our situation:

love seeking to enter into the experience of the objects of that love.

Sadly, only a minority realized that Jesus had come to show us the always-existing in the sphere of the temporary. He came to do a definite job, a rescue operation which was to launch the age of miracles.

## Love's Way

The coming to earth of Jesus our Lord certainly didn't "put everything right" in the way of visibly transforming human existence. He forecast that there was still much suffering for humanity to endure.

But what Jesus did was to help us to make more sense of this world with its huge contrasts of light and darkness. He gave us something to work on. He gave us a transforming potential for our lives, in a world where there is still so much unhappiness.

I think that the really wonderful thing which Jesus did was to show us how God could be found in the darkness. Without Jesus, millions of people, all honestly trying to look at life on earth, would still be in despair.

Jesus showed us, in those amazing three years, that there is a way for the dark places to be illuminated, and that He would continue to do this for us, if we'd only let Him. He showed us that even the darkness, although so painful for individuals, can serve God's long-term plans, plans which we could begin to see as love-motivated. There is a glimpse of this, of course, at the human level. Someone's "I love you" seems to have a greater intensity and meaning when spoken in a tragic or hostile environment.

\*　　\*　　\*

It was this wonderful love of Jesus which was the bridge between the permanent dimension and us often-confused human beings. When Jesus came, love was *expressed*. And love was *experienced* as never before. It was this love from which the miracles flowed, and still flow.

Although there may be some aspects of God becoming "one of us" in Jesus, which we can't grasp completely, it is obvious that He chose the logical way, the only effective way, to prove His indescribable love for us.

That love was making sure that He became part of us, and we part of Him. It was almost as if love couldn't stop itself from turning into a miracle!

## Into Focus

When writing this, I saw a lovely TV programme of Christian and Jewish people joining in "Songs of Praise" together. I'm sure that it brought home to all of us how much we have in common.

The only sad thing, for me, is that non-Christian faiths (to which many of my friends in hospital work belong) seem to miss so much, if Jesus is not bang in the centre of it all. As countless people will confirm, the risen Lord Jesus Christ somehow brings God's love into focus for us in this often cold-looking world.

As we look at Jesus, it's as if we see the light and the darkness, and all humanity's hopes and fears, actually meeting. As one mass-circulation Sunday newspaper once modestly said of itself, "All human life is there".

Each day I become more convinced, as I see what He means to people, that our Lord Jesus Christ is the clue to human existence. I believe that when we discover Jesus, we really start to find light in the darkness, we find God's resources, and we start to expect good things to happen. God's miracle-involvement, in fact, turns the changes we hope for from faint possibilities into probabilities!

Of course, there will be those who feel that "Life is all about Jesus" is merely a sweeping platitude. Well, let's see . . .

Millions still passionately believe that Jesus is God's instrument in the creative process. Our world is a sort of miraculous expression, in the material, of the love of God the Son. He made us!

Millions passionately believe, too, that Jesus came, at a definite point in history, not only to let the world see God, but very clearly to see Him *at work*.

It's as if Jesus our Lord was saying, "The One who brought you into being is letting you see – beyond a shadow of doubt – His love for you." Jesus's coming was somehow the starting point for all true spiritual knowledge.

And so, here is Jesus, a young man, eating, sleeping and always very much at risk. In Him, only the Divine love burns brightly. But far from being worshipped, He becomes the subject of growing sarcasm, scepticism and hatred – mainly from the religious leaders – those "professionals" again!

Jesus had come in order to experience, in the closest possible way, the sadness and disappointment, the sense of isolation, which can be involved in being a man or woman upon this earth. And His love is the reason that He has chosen to stay involved. This means that the caring presence is also a *feeling* one.

Jesus came to show us something vital: that God's purposes of helping us to feel loved are worked out in the most "impossible" places.

But what about today?

Through the risen Jesus, God watches over His world, but not now as a remote "wholly-other" Creator. He watches over us as a very loving Friend, to whom we can come with our sadness, our shattered dreams, and, yes, even our occasional anger about the sort of world He has given us. Jesus showed that being involved in creation, as we said earlier, means so much more than presiding over it and judging it.

Involved means what it says – a constant and loving influence (with interventions all the time) to bring order out of chaos, happiness out of bitterness.

\* \* \*

And so, it is through Jesus Christ that God the Father is so wonderfully at work . . . protecting us, rewarding us with a sense of His presence, making decisive changes in us, renewing us. He is constantly taking opportunities in people's lives, as well as letting them share in what He's doing.

Sad that He only gets "minority" recognition, but He must be used to that by now!

Jesus, our Lord, with that perfect combination of divine and human awareness, knows precisely how to step gently into the tangled circumstances of one of His children and to shape those circumstances into harmony. The things He does seem to stand out brilliantly, the more so because of the often-dark surroundings.

\* \* \*

Elizabeth dragged herself to the Chaplain's office, not really expecting very much after years of the blackest depressive spells. Elizabeth's problems had almost driven away her husband and family, and made her want to die, as the easiest solution.

Realizing what a stubborn case this was, as we sat there I could only silently offer the briefest "invitation" to Jesus to touch Elizabeth in some way. The conversation seemed to turn, in an uncanny fashion, to the subject of the love of Jesus, a thing which Elizabeth just about "believed in". I didn't realize it at the time, but this love was starting to light up in Elizabeth, who left the room after our chat looking much the same as when she came in.

Very shortly afterwards, Elizabeth was back – radiantly announcing that she was feeling so different and so grateful to God! Jesus had come to Elizabeth's rescue, and I was observing a quiet, and lasting, miracle. What a difference the genuine coming of Jesus always makes.

## Illuminated

Whenever there is an amazing peace found in a threatening situation, you can also find Jesus. Whenever we find things like courage emerging in those situations, there is Jesus. Even when there's apathy, or resistance, you can't stop Him lighting up places!

The light which Jesus brings is a kind of loving illumination of our whole life. If we live within that area of light we find wisdom, we find tranquillity, we find an ability to get on top of the things which used to defeat us. Once a person truly experiences Jesus lighting up his or her life, that person can never completely turn away from that light again.

By the illumination which Jesus brings we really see

ourselves for the first time (initially, it's painful, of course); but we begin, too, to see Him, and the light becomes an encouraging one! He brings a hope which we can't find anywhere else.

When life is illuminated by Jesus, it is as though all arguments stop, and there's just a sense of gratitude at having found something priceless. It is by the light of Jesus that we start to see God's miracle-work, enjoying the privilege of seeing what many have failed to see either because of pride, or of wanting to run their lives *their* way.

As we'll see later, when Jesus receives our confidence and our attention, miracles become a live subject! A stage is reached when even to think about Him in a crisis can bring about a miraculous change.

In hospitals, I see all the time the effect which Jesus (and only Jesus) has on those who have never been "religious". I see Him taking so many opportunities as people literally throw themselves, half-believing, on Him. All the time He is responding, as we stop trusting in acquired "knowledge" or in our moral "virtue", and just show a willingness to be His.

It makes such a difference when we know that Jesus touches life at every possible point, that He is at the heart of all existence, of every atom. It's not exaggerating to say that Jesus Christ is the Lord of History – at the centre of the whole drama of humanity, and its evolution. Without Jesus, so many people would have God as just an idea.

\* \* \*

Two thousand years ago a young man took the lifeless hand of a little girl, and a speechless Mother and Father saw her blink and then come back into their lives. *That* is Jesus, the light-bringer, and He's still very much at work.

There is much darkness still to be conquered, of course, many tears to be shed, as creation's purposes are worked out against huge opposition. But even where there's fierce resistance or complete apathy, Jesus, the light-bringer, ensures that God's purposes are marching forward all the time. Where there is a trusting expectancy, He makes you well and truly aware of that march!

All the time, people with tremendously varied temperaments and backgrounds are finding the world's darkness lighting up for them, finding themselves looking forward again . . . *as Jesus comes.*

# 4

# What Happened in Palestine?

In a few moments, when we look at Jesus's miracles, I'm sure that straightaway there'll be a nagging thought: "Dare I accept it all? Even the Church seems split about the things which Jesus did. Can I be sure?"

Yes, there is the sad situation in the second half of the twentieth century, that so many are diluting, or re-interpreting, or finding logical or "natural" explanations for all that Jesus did.

The number of "I-believe-in-God,-but . . ." people has grown frighteningly large! There is a world of difference, of course, between the wistful person who just cannot bring himself to believe the stories of Jesus, and those who feel that they have to dismiss first one miracle, then another, and to rule them out in the present day.

Many "radical" thinkers feel that God couldn't possibly upset the cause-and-effect system of law which He has created, and they are very cautious about some of the Palestinian miracles. It is an incredible thought that God, who made this planet out of love, should not demonstrate that love – for example, in the wonderful things which Jesus did. Much more likely the reverse!

Although God's involvement obviously doesn't mean causing absolute chaos by breaking divine laws, it does mean frequent loving activity of the kind Jesus showed us.

Sometimes I feel that we haven't really got hold of God's greatness . . . because of that greatness He is quite able to control, satisfactorily, the paradox of *His* power and *our* free will, existing side by side.

In a mysterious universe such as this, belief in God is, in itself, a tremendous thing. But why should it end there? Why should it all stop with a God who (in order not to break creative laws) remotely watches people making a terrible mess of their lives? It is surely a contradiction to talk about a loving God who just watches while the evolutionary process unfolds. Does He simply look on, with faint amusement, as we deceive ourselves that miracles are happening?

## Believable

"Of course I believe in God" sounds less and less convincing if it's coupled with shadowy "suspect" miracles, and an equally shadowy Jesus, who could have been mistaken about where He came from. To claim belief in God but then to talk and write as if the material and the "logical" are a little more real than the spiritual, is inconsistent.

If you have experienced the warm presence, the change-bringing presence, of Jesus in your life, it is hard to talk with the detachment of some of the more uncompromising radical thinkers. We must not accept that some of the things which occurred when God stepped into history have been proved to be myth, or legend, or exaggeration, *because they have not*!

It was Jesus's miracle-work, in fact, which gave the

only convincing answer so far to the question then asked, and still asked, "Is there any supernatural dimension to the universe?" I'm sure that the intuitive voice in us which confirms that there is a spiritual dimension, also tells us that we can trust the miracles as accurately reported!

I'm sure that (1) finding God in creation, (2) finding Him intuitively in our own hearts, and (3) seeing Him in the spectacular things which Jesus did, are all part of the same encounter. When one of these three carries a huge question-mark, the whole thing is weakened.

If there is a spiritual dimension to our existence, the miracles (free from all interpretations, watering-down and "explanations") are absolutely believable – walking on the water – everything!

The strongest argument by radical thinkers is that perhaps God would not have chosen some of the ways recorded. But if God exists, and if He broke into history in the person of Jesus, then the big surprise (in view of the need for it all to be unmistakable) would be if the spectacular things had *not* happened.

## A Power-Message

God's good news for the world simply had to be accompanied by a demonstration of His love and His power. Confronted by sickness, premature deaths, and despair, Jesus our Lord proceeded to show us the victory of God over material forces. He had to! In a poverty-stricken, disease-ridden corner of the Middle East, with an apparently absentee God, what Jesus did had to be so very convincing. You couldn't just "talk people into" belief in God, and how loving and powerful He was, otherwise people might have said (as Eliza Doolittle did in *My Fair Lady*), "Words, words . . . I'm so sick of words . . . *show* me!"

Jesus once sadly remarked, "Unless you see signs and wonders, you're not going to believe." And so He performed them – not to impress, but out of a burning love for each sad person with whom He was in contact.

We can see how necessary the miracles were when we read how, after some breathtaking act of healing, crowds of people became believers. It's difficult, too, to explain those many thousands of new converts, as the apostles journeyed around the Mediterranean, unless there had been some pretty remarkable events.

Far from being colourful inventions to brighten up the Good News, the miracles are in fact the base for proclaiming that news. Sceptics were knocked for six when Lazarus walked out of that tomb. Cynical onlookers became firm believers, within seconds, as Jesus changed people's situations. If some remarkable things hadn't occurred it is doubtful whether we would ever have heard the "message" of Jesus at all.

## Out of Balance

"For God's sake, use your reason", an ultra-radical thinker may remark, if you make him slightly angry by, say, your "naïve" belief in all the miracles.

Yes, of course he is right that, in the space age, the things which we believe should be able to stand intelligent and courageous investigation. The reasoning capacity which God gave us has to be used, and a reasoned faith, which has faced some of the hard facts, is usually a strong one. But how terribly out of balance the exaggerated use of reason, with its variety of "conclusions", has become.

Excessive freedom of interpretation can, sadly, lead many people to assume that the "difficult" miraculous event can be safely rejected. It's not such a huge step from having growing doubts about some of the events in the New Testament to doubts about God existing.

\* \* \*

Sometimes we are told that totally believing the wonderful things which Jesus did means that we're "conditioned" to accept them, rather as the Jewish people were.

I don't think we need to be too disturbed by this, because it's possible for the ultra-radical thinkers themselves to be a little "conditioned", although, of course, they feel that they are being intellectually honest.

Our judgements can often be coloured by an unfortunate "Western" materialism and empiricism. Because of the influences upon us of this "logical" Western thought, we don't always find it easy to accept the cosmic perspective of much that is recorded in the Bible.

Sadly, it is sometimes the case that scepticism and caution can be a protective covering to hide our personal spiritual disappointments. In a largely unconscious reasoning process, what we can be led into saying is, "It hasn't happened to me . . . therefore I don't think it's the sort of thing which ever *does* happen."

\* \* \*

When "logical" and somewhat sceptical arguments are used in support of an atheistic or agnostic viewpoint, that's fine. But it's sad when similar arguments are applied to events such as the miracles, and come from one or two ecclesiastical sources. The faith of thousands of would-be believers can be shattered before it has had time to find itself. When we broadcast our "conclusions" (often, anyway, disproved by later knowledge), we should pause to ask ourselves whether Jesus our Lord is being hurt by it, and whether many people are being deterred from taking even the first steps of trying to follow Him.

\*　　\*　　\*

Sometimes it is suggested by radical thinkers that the Bible tends to paint an idealized or exaggerated picture. Actually, most of the idealizing seems to occur today, with those beautiful nativity scenes, and the building up of certain Christian "personalities". But the Bible is brutally frank, showing us God at work in the midst of rivalries, crude mistakes by the disciples, and spiritual leaders with all sorts of personal defects – much nearer the true picture of Christianity today!

\*　　\*　　\*

So, once again, let us remember that God's breakthrough in Palestine took place in a crude and cruel setting favourable to atheism, and it had to be absolutely unmistakable. People just stood speechless as hope came back into the lives of the hopeless.

> Paralysed people suddenly leapt for joy.
> A young man restored to life, en route to his own funeral.
> Life-long blindness suddenly becoming a grateful look into Jesus's face.

An angry lake quietened by just a word.
Crazed individuals sent away in their right minds.

I'm sure we've said more than enough about belief and scepticism, and that we are ready to join Jesus, out there in the sun, and watch Him at work!

---

Dear Lord Jesus,

I have to listen to so many conflicting viewpoints in religious matters – please help my own faith to be a courageous one, not running away from facts.

As I read on, may I find a deep certainty about Yourself, and about the wonderful things which You can do for people today.

May this lead to Your growing involvement in every part of my life.

Thank You

---

# 5

# God's Plain Intention

"Oh, no, not yet another look at the miracles of Jesus!"

I can sympathize, because those miracles have been the subject of the most intense critical and devotional study. The reason for taking a good look at those New Testament miracles is an important one. We need to be sure of God's very plain intention to intervene . . . even to upset His own natural processes, where necessary!

Obviously, the eye-witnesses had an advantage over us, in experiencing the tangible and exciting ministry of Jesus. These eye-witnesses saw, beyond a shadow of doubt, that bringing healing and happiness was God's wish.

We need to have that deep certainty that God has exactly the same intention for us. That certainty will help us tremendously when, a little later, we study the ways (some of them often neglected) of getting ready for miracles.

I still hesitate slightly at plunging into those amazing three years in Palestine, because there are sure to be many who'll say wistfully, "I wish *that* could be me", as they read of someone being freed from a physical or emotional illness. But I think that we ought mentally to "follow Jesus around" (even if it can make us a little dissatisfied), because we can learn so much from those incidents to apply to our situations today.

It seems like a completely new experience each time we

read, with wonder and expectancy, about all that Jesus did. Our brief journey with Jesus won't be scholarly ("You can say that again", observes a critical reader), and I'm sure that it won't have scores of highly original insights. But it's always thrilling imaginatively to "be there" with Jesus, don't you think?

## Unmistakable

Jesus left people in no possible doubt that His ministry was one of power. He showed people not only God's willingness, but His eagerness to do something for them. The choice is a little overwhelming in picking out some of the marvellous things which Jesus did. And it's pretty certain, don't you think, that the choice would be even wider if we had had all the incidents reported? "There are many other things which Jesus did", says John. You bet! The miracles reported must be just a selection from hundreds of "incidents" in which human imperfection and unhappiness came into contact with the love and power of God, through Jesus.

Nearly all the happenings centred upon Jesus are in the "Phew, look at that!" category. People realized that they were seeing things which had never been seen before and which they were unlikely to see again.

For many people, "quiet" miracles would not have been enough. Someone saying, "I feel a lot happier since Jesus spoke to me", might have been accused of putting on an act. Many of the things which Jesus did for people were, therefore, spectacular, and left no room for doubt.

Why did Jesus do all these things? Why did He move

about, so unerringly, making people well and happy again?

Well, firstly, it was to express the clear will of God about human sadness, and the various human limitations. The Kingdom of God had come with Jesus, and that Kingdom represents light and joy. Jesus had good news to give us and He demonstrated it. Secondly, there was our Lord's incredible compassion. He just couldn't help reaching out in love. Thirdly, the things which He did were to show that He was, in fact, the Person they had all been waiting for: the Divine Son, the world's Saviour.

With these things as the base from which He worked, Jesus proceeded to immerse Himself in the opportunities all around Him. "That's Me", he said, when pointing to Isaiah's reference to One with the Spirit of God resting on Him, setting people free.

And so Jesus travelled about, opening the eyes of both the spiritually and physically blind, and setting free those who were locked up in fear and despair. Not only were there many physical cures, of course, but instances of what would today be called "inner healing" – broken hearts mended.

The nature of the person's trouble, or its duration, became irrelevant, as is the case today when God steps in to change longstanding situations. Those people who met Jesus were lifted out of earth's limitations – and anything was possible at that moment.

The very presence of Jesus our Lord provoked a child-like expectancy in so many, even including one or two of the rabbis! It is this same expectancy which leads to miracles in the twentieth century, too.

\*     \*     \*

For a long time now, the miracles of Jesus have been put into roughly four categories, though it's doubtful whether He, or anyone else, bothered to see them that way! But, anyway, these categories are to show God's power over:

1. Disease
2. Personalized supernatural evil
3. Forces of nature
4. Death

The first two categories do, of course, overlap a little, because, as we know, Jesus often got rid of some evil interference just before (or simultaneously with) physical healing. There's a lovely little group of miracles which were in response to some people's sheer pestering and determination, throwing embarrassment to the wind and almost *demanding* that Jesus did something for them (we're going to look at one or two of these).

All the miracles – whatever their "category" – make exciting reading. As we follow Jesus around, I know that we'll be able to draw from them great encouragement in meeting our present problems.

By the way, I thought we might follow the example of Dorothy Sayers in her famous play – *The Man Born To Be King* – and take the liberty of giving names to some of the characters who came into contact with Jesus.

Lord Jesus . . .

I am going to sit back for a while now and look again at the things which You did. Help me to watch those things with a sense of wonder. As I watch, may it result in my becoming a good present-day subject for the miraculous.

Thank You

# 6

# The Irresistible Combination

The streets of the towns and villages which we now walk
with Jesus so often resemble an open-air hospital. Disease, handicap, insanity, simply scream out at us. The
sun may be shining, but in most other ways the setting is
a dark one.

Much of the illness is, of course, congenital. The
sufferers have known nothing else, only years of despair.
Certainly most of the trouble is far too deep-seated to be
dealt with by strong "suggestion", or by the removal of a
temporary psychosomatic cause.

### Unconventional Love

Don't you like the encouragement given to all
longstanding sufferers as we move, with Jesus, towards
that helpless-looking man at the Pool of Bethesda?

Thirty-eight years! Yes, most of his life longing for a
miracle. It's Simeon. Learning of the long duration of
Simeon's illness, Jesus, as usual, wastes no words. "Get
up! Pick up your mat, and start walking, Simeon." Instantaneously (we encounter that word quite a lot!)
Simeon does as he's told, and amazes everyone.

Here is God's power simply asserting itself. No long

prayers, no urging, no pretence, just someone getting better on the spot. Soon afterwards we meet Simeon again for a moment. No need for our Lord to ask, "How are you feeling?" He just joyfully confirms it all for Simeon by saying, "See . . . you're well now."

Obviously the circumstances of this particular incident don't apply to most of us . . . or do they? There are hundreds of thousands today who are able to say that Jesus has "put right" some very longstanding problem, physical or emotional. He does what is needed thoroughly – and it lasts!

There are quite a few confrontations with those "non-respectable" people who have leprosy. Here's Reuben.

"Lord, I'm pretty sure that, if You're willing, it will be no problem for You to get rid of this thing for me."

Well, how could our Lord resist that?

As we watch Jesus with Reuben we see two vital things involved in the relationship of the risen Jesus with us today: (1) His compassion and (2) His identification with us.

So many of the things we see Jesus doing as we follow Him around are that beautiful and irresistible combination of compassion and power.

"Lord, if You're willing . . ."

"Willing? Yes, of course I am, Reuben."

Then, of course, Jesus does the unthinkable thing. He *touches* the man with leprosy . . . in a society in which you just don't go within a quarter of a mile of such a person if you can help it.

That touch of Jesus is a supreme example of His unconventionality – sweeping aside all the man-made customs. That touch is one of fellow feeling with the sufferer. Knowing how Jesus took the children in His arms, I can just imagine Him putting an arm around Reuben's shoulder for a moment or two, can't you? "Of course I'm willing, my friend." In any event, the man's repulsive condition disappears instantaneously (that word again!)

As we watch Jesus, it's beginning to dawn on us that His miracles are really love in action. His love towards one of His children who will turn trustingly to Him is a guarantee of forces directed towards the help, in some way, of that person.

## Blindness – of Both Kinds!

What a lot of eye afflictions there seem to be. Those pious people around us seem to think that not seeing is a punishment for something in the life of the sufferer, or perhaps that of his parents. Here's Benjamin . . . a lifetime's blindness.

"Tell us, Jesus, what's this a punishment for?" say the onlookers.

"It's not a punishment at all", He quietly replies. It's as if He's answering the agonized question of so many of us today when misfortune strikes! "Why should this have to happen to me?"

The blindness in Benjamin's particular case, and confronted on this particular day, is so that God's power might be demonstrated for everyone to see.

Explanations over, Jesus performs one of His slightly slower miracles! We know the incident well, don't we? Jesus smears mud on Benjamin's eyes, and tells him to go and wash in the pool some distance away. This miracle needs a faith-response from Benjamin. Fortunately, he doesn't irritably wipe away the mud! Benjamin goes to the pool and does as he's told.

Benjamin finds, of course, that there is the sky, there are the trees, and there are those human shapes to match up to the voices he already knows.

What a storm this particular miracle arouses! The religious professionals, in their spiritual blindness, grill Benjamin about the manner of the healing, and even interview his parents. "Yes, he's our son", they say. Jesus is cutting across the presuppositions of the "experts" about the way in which they feel God should work. And they don't like it.

Benjamin is getting a bit tired of all these questions about Jesus, and, with a lovely piece of sarcasm, says to the priestly questioners: "Perhaps you want to be His disciples, too!"

The growing and sinister enmity of the religious leaders causes them to cast doubt upon our Lord's person. "Give God the credit for this, not Jesus."

The questioning eventually brings Benjamin's exasperated and marvellous reply (possibly applying to some of the present-day sceptics?), "I don't really know about Jesus and His character . . . One thing, however, I do know: I was blind, and now I can see!"

Jesus bumps into Benjamin again shortly afterwards. Benjamin says devotedly, "Lord, I believe in You." How could he do anything else?

There are many who slightly "demote" Jesus today. They cast doubt upon His words, and generally tend to take away His uniqueness (listen to some of the more trendy sermons). But Benjamin, and the more open-minded in the crowd, know on this day that if this isn't God at work in Jesus, they might as well all become non-believers.

Here is a joyful event. The professionals "see" it, but fail to see it. It doesn't fit into their scheme of things. Can the hostility also be covering up a feeling of guilt – that God is not doing through them the sort of thing He has just done for Benjamin?

Yes, the priests and lawyers fail to see what they are "seeing", and the danger of making the same mistake about the things which God is doing for so many people today is obvious.

\* \* \*

As we watch Jesus, we see God's power simply pouring from Him, as almost an automatic response to need. This deaf man hearing the birds again, and uttering his first words after the command "Be opened!" The usual large crowd overwhelmed once again – and saying among themselves, "He makes a good job of everything!"

We peep inside the local synagogue, and there's another hostile group. It is the Sabbath, and they are watching to see whether Jesus will step out of line. He does! Angry at their bigotry and hardness, He defiantly commands a shrivelled-up arm to straighten itself out, and one can only guess at the course of the service afterwards.

Finally, here's a two-stage miracle – which may be an encouragement for the many today whose progress is gradual. Our Lord takes a blind man apart from the crowd and lays His hands on the man's eyes.

"Do you see anything?"

"Well, I can see what look like trees walking around!"

Then Jesus again puts His hands on the man's eyes and vision becomes perfect.

The experience of so many today who have sought healing is that more than one Divine "touch", more than one prayer encounter, may be needed. The healing process may be a gradual one, but Jesus our Lord sees to it that the period involved, though calling for patience, is not going to be a wasted one.

## Re-discovered

Watching Jesus in action could, as we said, make many of us wistful, especially those who are longing for miracles for ourselves. It's tremendously encouraging, though, that towards the end of the twentieth century Jesus's power seems to be in the process of being re-discovered . . . at last!

The power is by no means flowing as it could, through His still imperfect instruments, but healings and changed personalities are no longer surprises. The way in which God takes the opportunities which our trusting lives offer Him amazes us more each day.

The incredible healing of sick people in Palestine is thought by many to be Jesus "acting out" a sort of forecast for us. He is giving us a glimpse into the future when God's power will put an end to all human suffering.

Shall we follow Jesus a little further? We're going to see Him involved in an unavoidable and decisive confrontation.

Lord,

It's always exciting to watch You at work . . . making drawn faces break into smiles.

But please don't let it end there. May Your work among those sick people do something in me. Let me have a deep conviction of Your being able to achieve anything. Let me, from now, have a real and growing sense of *expectancy*.

Thank You

# 7

# The Right Diagnosis

We can read the stories of Jesus in a way-out paraphrase by a most "advanced" thinker. We may even try reading them with one eye closed, or even standing on our head. But whichever way we read about what Jesus did, I think that we'll find it impossible to escape one conclusion: here is a tremendous confrontation between God and evil forces.

People who are, literally, being destroyed, find themselves free and happy again, after Jesus has made the right diagnosis, and applied God's power to their situation.

It's not fashionable in many places (some of them ecclesiastical) to speak of personalized forces of evil, but as we read thoughtfully about what Jesus did, we shall, I know, become increasingly sure of their existence.

It is wrong to try to remove from the scene those intangible but very real forces which Jesus was up against, and which His extreme sensitivity always detected – hence the miracles! Later in the book we'll look at how recognition of those forces (without becoming morbidly preoccupied with them) can today start changing defeated personalities into victorious ones.

And so, here is Jesus, before making someone well again, having to confront an evil entity. Somehow, evil has forced an entry into a life, and Jesus our Lord has to deal with this "presence". All the time we see Jesus engaged in very real warfare, pushing back the influence of evil in people's lives.

It sometimes seems as if the main purpose of our Lord being on the earth is to signal to people the defeat of these forces of evil. The insights of psychosomatic medicine tend to show us that the recognition by Jesus of some "diabolical interference" behind a physical illness is not as far-fetched as many used to think.

Although evil may not be able directly to affect our physical functions, it can of course infiltrate our mental processes, building up a dark and negative emotional life, from which all sorts of illnesses can come. This process would account for many of the sad cases which Jesus encountered.

\*     \*     \*

Here's young Isaac, with what would seem to be symptoms of particularly bad epilepsy, brought by his Dad. The father explains that this is his only child, and one can imagine the hell which the boy's loved ones have lived through when one listens to the father's story. Isaac is in the habit of screaming, throwing himself about, getting into water or near fire. "Whatever it is," comments his father accurately, "it is literally destroying the boy."

But this is to be the happiest day in the life of Isaac and in the lives of his family, because a young man called Jesus is within reach!

Our Lord diagnoses the situation. Isaac is the victim of an unseen force, to which Jesus gives an order to "Go!" The boy convulses violently, and then Jesus takes him gently by the hand, having restored him to quietness and normality.

Isaac's rescue is carried out with the usual immediacy, of course, and with the now familiar gasp from the onlookers about "the greatness of God".

Poor Abigail. This lady has an apparent spinal curvature, more severe than most. Quite unable to straighten up, Abigail is noticed by Jesus in a synagogue service. Jesus looks round at those nearby. "She's in a prison – created by evil", He explains.

It is a more hostile and defensive "audience" this time. Putting His hands on Abigail Jesus tells her, "You're set free." Immediately Abigail straightens up, now looking at the sky rather than at her feet. We notice that Abigail's spirit is set free as well. She praises God, and no doubt disturbs the orderly conduct of yet another service.

We find a case here of Jesus noticing a need, without, apparently, being approached by this lady. We are reminded of how often in the lives of those who trust Him today Jesus, the risen Lord, moves to meet needs we have barely recognized, or about which we haven't even sought His help!

\*     \*     \*

It's interesting to see how almost identical miracles produce such widely differing reactions. It seems incredible that many of our Lord's miracles (which are merely making the world a happier place again for someone) should produce the reactions which they do.

The ecclesiastical people feel threatened. They feel that Jesus represents blasphemy against a God whom *they* clearly don't come within a million miles of knowing! This Jesus is playing up to the ignorant and credulous riff-raff, ignoring proper religious order and decency. When you're threatened as badly as that, you feel justified in plotting to kill!

As we said earlier, there are many today who produce all sorts of "explanations" and "coincidences" to account for the miraculous. Things which should thrill them virtually become non-events.

It seems as if there will always be two opposing reactions of (1) wonder and excitement, and (2) sceptical reserve, whenever God lets a little light into our existence!

\*     \*     \*

We notice that sometimes Jesus "rebukes" an illness. There is this element of rebuke, even in what seems a homely problem like Peter's mother-in-law with a fever and unable to prepare the meal. This again suggests that the acutely-sensitive perception of Jesus detected some personalized activity of evil.

Isn't it wonderful to notice, here and there, how the gospel writers describe miracles as almost something you just take for granted if Jesus is present? For example, with great economy of words, Matthew reports how a man in the grip of an evil spirit, and unable to talk, is brought along. Then in the next breath, Matthew almost nonchalantly says, "*When* the evil spirit was driven out, the man began to talk." Matthew permits himself to record the crowd's response that "nothing like this has ever been seen in our country".

Another almost casual piece of reporting, from the same writer, is about a man who had a double incapacity. Just three lines dispose of this incident, which might need a chapter in a present-day book. Listen to this:

"They brought a man, possessed by a spirit, who was blind and dumb, and Jesus healed him, so that he could both talk and see."

That's it! The usual sureness of touch in confronting evil, and this means that the Good News, accompanied by signs of God's power, just can't help spreading like wildfire.

\*     \*     \*

Provoked by the presence of Jesus at a synagogue service, the evil spirit in a man causes a disturbance by yelling, "Have you come to destroy us, Jesus?" "Shut up," says Jesus, "and come out!"

It's the authority of Jesus in dealing with evil manifestations which leaves the onlookers almost speechless. It would be hard to account for these remarkable incidents by saying that these were mere personality disorders, brought to someone with great powers of "suggestion".

These encounters with evil show what always happens when the rule of God is brought up against the power which is working to frustrate that rule.

Isn't it exciting to realize that there are great untapped cosmic forces all around us, forces far stronger than evil? The world's Saviour – then and now – is the point of contact for those forces. No localized "wonder worker", but the channel through whom God's creative and restoring power is released to us.

\*     \*     \*

There are, of course, many other instances to remind us of what we so often find today: that where there is a genuine attempt to follow Jesus, there goes with it a heightened awareness of a force trying to wreck the whole process. If this force is ignored, or underestimated, we're likely to be in spiritual danger.

However, these New Testament incidents remind us of something else: that the power represented by Jesus will always win! It's the power of *love*, and will ultimately bring about a total cosmic victory.

If only we realized how many times in a day followers of Jesus are rescued from physical and moral dangers, how often we are saved from the consequences of our own blindness, as Jesus our Lord frustrates the strategy of evil in our lives.

I'm sure that one of the reasons why forces of evil are permitted their continued activity is that they, in fact, provide opportunities for God. Evil's strategy can be forced to play a part in God's own plans for us. Conditions brought about by the influence of evil can make us realize the fear potential, and the emptiness, of life without God. This is, so often, God's opportunity to increase our sense of dependency upon Him, and to unite our existence a little closer with His own.

---

Dear Lord,

It's not easy to "prove" the existence of personal evil in the universe, opposed to You. But I realize that unless I share Your clear belief, there is a dimension lacking in my own thinking about the miraculous.

Without becoming morbid or obsessional about evil, help me nevertheless to recognize its reality. Help me to take evil's power seriously – but also to remember that Your power is greater! As I come to terms with this problem, I know I will start to experience miracles in my own life.

# 8

# Nature Obeys

Jesus came to show that God is in charge.

The so-called "nature miracles" are just as easy to believe as the healing miracles, don't you think? No need to explain or "re-interpret", if this is the Creator in the midst of the environment He has brought into being. No need to regard the nature miracles as colourful embellishments to the Gospel stories, if God is, for a special purpose, visiting this planet.

It's interesting that in about four of the nature miracles, Jesus our Lord is doing a kindness.

The first kind act is that incredible provision of connoisseur's wine for the embarrassed host at the wedding reception. I'm sure that Jesus must be at many gatherings, often in the company of "outsiders" (as the priests see them). The warmth and magnetism of His humanity surely make Him good to be with. The Divine nature, for its part, is quite capable of meeting any emergency, as the wine-provision shows. An opportunity beautifully taken . . . and the festivities can continue!

There's an obvious lesson for us in Jesus producing the best wine at the end, isn't there?

Life, for a majority, gets gradually a little harder, of course, as age increases. But countless people have found that with Jesus the process can be reversed. As our acquaintance with Him grows, we realize that we can eagerly anticipate what He has planned for us.

## Emergencies

We don't know exactly how many times our Lord "obliged" when His friends had failed to catch any fish, but we're pretty sure of two such occasions, one before, and one after His resurrection. In one incident, probably without expecting very much, the heavy-eyed disciples dutifully let down the nets when requested and just can't cope with the catch.

I am forcibly reminded of how the Lord so wonderfully provides for His trusting children today . . . answering prayers with just what is needed . . . and, as we often find later, at exactly the right moment.

Over and over again, Jesus rescues us from the desperate situations in which we find ourselves – or into which, sometimes deliberately, we get ourselves.

Perhaps we can picture ourselves on board that frail boat on Galilee Lake. Again, a very familiar incident, with Jesus having forty winks while the storm rages. A furious storm – almost as if nature is getting out of hand. When Jesus is awakened, we notice that He first "rebukes" the wind and the sea. Some thoughtful commentators feel that the "rebuking" indicates that there might well be some cosmic and personal force of evil at work when the forces of nature run riot. "Stop it!" commands this amazing character whom we have on board. And there is a great calm.

"Even the wind and the waves do what He tells them", say the disciples. Of course!

Why should this incident be even remotely considered

as a legend? It's even harder to believe that in such a situation the very agent in the creative process would be powerless.

Yes, a risky universe, and, to be honest, we sometimes feel very much at the mercy of its forces. We wish, perhaps, that God would intervene a little more often. But we can be sure that the last word *is* with God. The message of the storm-calming is that in God's care we are still "at risk" – but ultimately safe.

*    *    *

Yet another loving act on a huge scale is that favourite passage for the present-day radical "interpreters", the feeding of the crowd.

"Just everyone sharing their picnic lunches", say some of the advanced expositors in theological journals, and even from pulpits. Yes, it is an incredible incident, but why try to find a "natural" explanation?

Let's consider, for a moment, the suggestion that everyone present shared their picnic lunches. It has probably struck many readers already that not everyone in the crowd thronging around Jesus on this day is obligingly carrying a picnic lunch – very few, I would imagine.

A little boy's lunch is used for this miracle, but if the gospel writers had wanted to make it even more breathtaking, they would surely have said that Jesus fed the crowd out of nothing! Don't you feel, as I do, that the story has the strong sense of authenticity?

Shortly after feeding the crowd and having quite a lot of food left over, Jesus finds many of them still following Him.

"You're only following Me because you were fed a few

minutes ago!" He says. Well, they would hardly be following Him because of some great non-event like the sharing of their picnic lunches. The feeding of the crowd is surely just our Lord's compassion, and His God-power, responding to a very natural situation.

Many feel that the feeding of the crowd was another "acted prophecy", pointing to the day when eventually all human needs will be met. Anyway, it's one more rather spectacularly taken opportunity.

## Peter's Experiment

Having watched Jesus during this breathtaking period, most of us would be reluctant to share the critics' suspicions about a further happening – His walking on the lake.

The crowd-feeding, the huge catches of fish, the wine-provision, the storm-quietening, and now His defiance of gravity on Galilee, seem to hang beautifully together – simply God intervening in our world of nature, to leave people in no possible doubt that there is another dimension.

Don't you love the little glimpse, in Matthew's version, of Peter with a chance of copying this miraculous feat, but messing it up? The miracle is within his grasp but, as they say, he "blows" it.

"Don't be afraid", Jesus says to His friends as He comes across the water to them. Peter (who else?) impulsively wants to do the same as his Master. "All right, come on then, Peter."

Peter could have been talked about for years afterwards as the fisherman who actually *walked* on Galilee as well as fished in it. But, after a successful step or two, Peter takes his eyes off Jesus and looks at the sea. End of experiment. I'm sure that this story was passed on by Peter, a story against himself, and one of the many places in the Bible where you're conscious of real truth, rather than invention-to-impress. An invented incident would surely have left out the part about sinking.

A little later we're going to look at how the atmosphere for miracles is created when we start keeping our eyes on Jesus, and how very difficult things can become when, like Peter, we don't.

---

Lord Jesus,

Thank You for the glimpse (and it was only a glimpse) of the power which the Father exercised through You in the creative process.

Let this certainty that You are *in control* – even though events do seem, temporarily, to get out of hand – make me unafraid.

---

# 9

# Embarrassing, But . . .

Among the people helped by Jesus was a group of desperate ones who just wouldn't take "no" for an answer. They saw an opportunity to be helped – and hoped that Jesus would do the same! These were people who were prepared even to make a public exhibition of themselves, if necessary. Here they are:

Bartimaeus.
Four anonymous stretcher-carriers.
The woman who jostled through a crowd.
Zacchaeus.
A Roman officer.
A nobleman.
A mother with a non-Jewish background.

A lovely, incongruous little group. Perhaps we can identify with the needs of one or two of them. Perhaps, too, we can learn something from them about our present situations.

Let's consider dear old Bartimaeus, one of the familiar sights in Jericho, fed up with begging at the roadside because of his blindness. Well, Bartimaeus certainly makes an exhibition of himself, doesn't he?

"Jesus . . . JESUS! . . . have mercy on me!"

"Shut up . . . it's embarrassing", say people nearby.

Undeterred, Bartimaeus throws caution to the wind. "Jesus . . . JESUS! Have mercy on me!" (Louder than before, and loud enough for our Lord to stop in His tracks.)

"Bring him to Me."

All at once, Bartimaeus becomes respectable! "Would you mind coming this way, Bartimaeus? The Master would like to see you."

Soon Bartimaeus is looking into the eyes of the Saviour of the world, having left his shut-in existence. In wonder and gratitude, Bartimaeus joins the crowd following Jesus.

Here's Matthias, badly paralysed, finding the most unorthodox way of securing Jesus's attention. We'll never know whose idea it is to break up the roof – but in any event Matthias is past caring about what people think. His four friends, with grim determination (and possibly with protests from the house-owner), lower Matthias down to the feet of Jesus. Matthias's spectacular arrival, and his faith, are more than the compassion of Jesus can resist. But first our Lord has to deal with unforgiven wrong things in Matthias's life. This may well be sparking off the thought in the stretcher-carriers' minds, "This wasn't exactly what we had in mind for Matthias!" But our Lord has to show that He is not merely concerned with putting bodies right, but putting *people* right. It is an uncomfortable few minutes for the religious leaders – first the dramatic intrusion, and then Jesus pronouncing for-giveness ("Just who does He think He is?") The question is convincingly answered when Matthias gets up and walks away! The Divine authority and the Divine healing-power were there, in Jesus, for the world to see.

In so many incidents, we can trace this instinctive response of Jesus to the desperate.

## Only a Touch

It must be far from easy for our friend Zillah, the lady with the longstanding haemorrhage, to push through to the Person who represents her last hope.

"Stop shoving" . . . but, like Bartimaeus, she knows that this is her great opportunity. Here is amazing faith: that just to make an anonymous contact with Jesus can solve everything. And it does. Realizing that one touch in this jostling crowd has been purposeful, our Lord tells an apologetic Zillah that she can go home cured.

It's interesting that Zillah isn't the only one to touch Jesus expectantly. Matthew reports the healing of many people who made this sort of contact with our Lord.

\*     \*     \*

Don't you have a soft spot for Zacchaeus? A corrupt little tax-man, hated by the people, but with a great hunger in his heart. And so Zacchaeus makes that undignified ascent of a tree to get a good view of Jesus, almost certainly earning derision from the crowd in the process. But he doesn't care.

Then comes the life-changing moment. Jesus looks up and says, "Zacchaeus, come on down, and let's talk!"

"How on earth can Jesus know my name . . . ?"

I'm pretty sure that the miracle of Zacchaeus's changed life happened before he came down from the tree. Don't you think that it dated from the speaking of his name?

The physical cures got the headlines, of course, but let's not forget the many character-changes, like that of Zacchaeus, which Jesus produced. There is no evidence of any dramatic healing for any of the disciples, for example, but oh, what changed personalities among them! The love of Jesus was much more than an attitude – it was an influence. You might almost say that things began to change as soon as He looked at you.

## At a Distance

You don't fraternize too much with those inferior Jews if you are a representative of imperial Rome, especially one in a position of seniority. But don't you admire our friend the centurion? He, too, doesn't care what people think. He approaches this "Jewish preacher" about his sick servant in wonderful humility and faith. The result is another of our Lord's "miracles at a distance", which seem just as effortless as those in which there is physical contact with the afflicted person. We increasingly feel as we "watch" Him, that with Jesus *everything* is possible.

We can note the consistent flow of Jesus's power in response to that abandonment on the part of people who came to Him. Sometimes it's a trust-born-of-desperation, but it's trust just the same. There is a letting-go of pride, a letting-go of all other hopes . . . and it's this to which our Lord is responding.

Making the journey from Capernaum to Cana in order to get to Jesus is another desperate man – an officer in the royal household.

You don't worry about Herod, or the Pharisees, or anyone else when your boy is dying. As with the Roman officer, our Lord gives a reassuring word without going to see the patient.

"You may go. Your son will live."

The royal official takes Jesus at His word, and soon overjoyed servants run to meet him with the news that his son is well. The father realizes that the time at which his son got better was exactly that at which Jesus had said his boy would live.

No wonder the whole of that official's household become believers!

Just one more example of desperate determination. This is the Greek lady who finds out where Jesus is staying, and dares to argue with Him when He suggests that His primary mission at that time is to the Jewish people.

"Even the dogs under the table eat the crumbs which fall", she neatly replies, and is rewarded by the setting free of her evil-possessed daughter.

What Jesus is doing, of course, soon has the nation talking. "He does everything perfectly", is one comment – and a very suitable one to apply to the changes He has brought about in people over the past two thousand years.

Although Jesus doesn't *need* us to make the perfect conditions for Him to act, we can see clearly that there is a miracle-potential whenever a person – in New Testament days or now – leaves behind all other "props", and throws himself or herself on Jesus.

We see Jesus cutting right across temperament and background, just as He does today. There is a unique opportunity-situation when there is that compelling, almost desperate, sense of personal need combined with an instinct that Jesus is the only answer.

Dear Lord,

Please help me to be single-minded. Help me to get rid of temporary "solutions" and compromises, and just bank on You. May I see You as the answer to every need which may arise, to know that some good *must* come from seeking Your help.

And, Lord, let others see my reliance upon You – a reliance which always brings miracles closer.

Thank You

# 10

# The Ultimate Challenge

We don't know how many people mentioned in the New Testament would have died without the intervention of Jesus. Certainly, quite a considerable number who were very close to dying, did recover dramatically. But what about those people who have actually died? They, of course, present Jesus with His greatest challenge. No hope of auto-suggestion here, no unlocking of psychosomatic symptoms, no "faith-response". Just corpses!

\*     \*     \*

Those parents who have lost an only child will identify with that poor lady in the village of Nain. Her only son, Baruch, very prematurely dead. In a country where life is cheap, here is yet another funeral procession, without any of the trimmings and privacy of today.

But we know now, of course, that there happens to be in town this day a remarkable young man in whom people are beginning to see the mysterious God. "Happens" is used advisedly, because this crossing of the paths of Jesus and grieving mother is no mere coincidence.

Jesus moves straight to the mother and says, "Don't

cry." Once more, that wonderful combination of compassion and power is seen. Jesus asks the coffin-bearers to stand still for a moment.

"Baruch, I say to you, 'Get up!'"

Sitting up in the coffin, Baruch begins to talk – his first words possibly being, "What's going on?" Jesus gives Baruch back to his overjoyed mother. Light breaks into the experience of those who see it all happen. They are filled with wonder, and praise God. More converts!

*       *       *

Jairus is a very respected figure in the religious world, and may be tempted to feel himself compromised by approaching the controversial Jesus. Jairus could be making himself less than popular with the hard-liners! But if your little girl is dying, there's only one thing to do when there's someone like Jesus around.

And so Jairus ignores what the onlookers might think and forsakes his dignity actually to fall at the feet of our Lord! . . .

"*Please* come and put Your hands on Susannah so that she will live, Jesus."

During the walk to Jairus's house, as we know, the chilling message comes: "It's too late . . . Susannah has died."

Can you imagine Jesus gripping Jairus's arm as He says, "Now don't be afraid . . . just go on believing"? Jesus presses through – ignoring the "realism" of the onlookers in a setting where infant mortality is very high.

In a wonderful few moments at the bedside, Susannah is given back to her overjoyed Mum and Dad. It's not difficult to picture the quiet joy on our Lord's face when a little girl comes back to life, the whispered "Thank

You" to the heavenly Father. A quiet joy which we can be sure the risen Jesus feels today whenever He can take an opportunity to bring happiness back into someone's life.

## A Friend Dies

Nowhere more than in the restoring to life of Lazarus in the village of Bethany can we see so clearly the overflowing empathy of Jesus.

Lazarus is a great friend and so, when he falls ill, his sisters simply send the message, "Lord, the one whom You love is sick." As we know, Jesus doesn't exactly hurry to the sick bed. Lazarus dies, leaving his sisters, Martha and Mary, shattered. In the meantime, Jesus confides to His disciples: "Our friend Lazarus has fallen asleep. I'm going there to wake him up . . . For your sakes, in order that you might believe, I'm glad I wasn't there when it happened."

"Wake him up? What next?"

When Jesus gets to Bethany, Lazarus has already been in the tomb for four days, and his sisters go as near as they can to telling Jesus that He might have been a little quicker off the mark. But this is the key moment in the lives of Martha and Mary. Such is the faith which the very presence of Jesus arouses that Martha and Mary still think that there can be a miracle.

And so there is. We notice that this is no mere local "faith-healer" who now walks towards the cave with Martha and Mary. The love from which the miracles flowed is obvious, as the very human Jesus shares in the family grief, and unaffectedly weeps for Lazarus. A really authentic note, surely.

Then . . . the power! A command to move away the stone (which is obeyed, if incredulously). A moment or two of prayer (merely following up what had been earnestly prayed about days previously), and then the shout of "Come out, Lazarus!"

Lazarus, still in his grave-clothes, of course, emerges. There is the usual result: many of the onlookers become firm believers from now on. Hard not to! And how could Mary and Martha ever forget, even temporarily, this particular act of God?

\*      \*      \*

There are occasional reports today, from various parts of the world, that a prayer at a bedside has meant a recovery, even from apparent death. Clearly, the most thorough investigations are needed, but as a Christian doctor in Britain said recently, "I don't think you can rule it out, if the Divine power was somehow getting through!"

In any event, Jesus showed us beyond doubt that death need not be final, that God really does have it in His power to give life again, even if this has to be in some new realm of existence.

Outside that cave Jesus made a comment to Martha which was surely meant for each one of us, so that it might burn into us: "Anyone who believes in *Me*, even if he dies, can *expect* to go on living!" As we recognize the power of Jesus within the details of our lives, we realize that this is no empty promise.

Dear Lord,

I can't escape, for very long, from the realization of my impermanence. When I ask for whom the bell tolls, the answer is uncomfortable. There's nowhere else to look but to You, for even the smallest clue about survival. Thank You that Your miracles, and Your own resurrection, give me just enough to hold on to . . . in the midst of the faith-destructive phenomena of life.

What a lot of hope is brought back into people's lives during that amazing three-year ministry, not only for those made well again, but for literally thousands of spectators too!

People who are a burden to themselves, and to others.
People near to death.
People already dead.

And then, of course, there was Mary Magdalene.

# 11

# Our Miracles Begin Here

Mary was herself a walking miracle. She had, as we know, been involved in a despised way of life, destined only for a dead end. Mary had found a completely new direction under the influence of Jesus. It seems that she arrived at a spiritual awareness which made some of the men disciples look a bit ordinary! A bit of "women's lib" two thousand years ahead of its time?

Anyway, who better to stand beside as we look, for a moment or two, at those tremendous events occurring within three days of each other?

\* \* \*

Mary was, I'm sure, standing as close to the Cross as she possibly could. With Mary, we look up at the young man who, only weeks ago, was radiantly, powerfully, changing people's lives. Now, here is a dishevelled and weak leader of a discredited and defeated cause, inviting only sarcasm or half-pitying amusement. But as we look up at Jesus we're seeing a miracle, aren't we? As those minutes tick by in the darkness, there is victory being won. A victory is being won by love and apparent weakness over brute force and hatred. It is the great "crunch" moment of history between hell-let-loose and God's love.

Through her tears, Mary would not yet realize that she was seeing something miraculous before her Easter morning experience. The Cross was a miracle just as wonderful as those performed by Jesus among the dying and the evil-tormented. With Mary, we're watching the life-giver actually giving away His own life! We're watching Jesus, in His perfection, letting Himself bear all the pride, the selfishness, and the hardness which can be in us. Here was Jesus identified with the sense of apartness-from-God which people's wrong ways can bring on them.

Wasn't it a huge gamble which the love of Jesus took? If that gamble hadn't been taken, we would never have heard of miracles. If that gamble hadn't been taken, we would almost certainly not be here, two thousand years later, discussing it all.

## The Driving-Force

As we look at the Cross it's as if we are seeing a summing-up of all that God wants to do for His children. Here was history's opportunity for God's love to show just how victorious it can be. In this love-victory we see the pattern of what Jesus our Lord aims to do in *all* our lives — to bring light into the dark places. It's a permanent victory, even though evil influences continue (as Jesus forecast they would). Later we'll see how Jesus's love is the driving-force behind miracles today, and how it guarantees His intervention in our own lives.

The love seen in the gloom on the hill outside Jerusalem just goes on . . . and on . . . That love is eager to identify with any person's desperate need.

As Alex lay dying in a hospital ward, he whispered to

me, with tears in his eyes, "He's still suffering with us today, isn't He?"

Yes, Alex, the suffering love of Jesus is extended to embrace us now. This is because He became, and always will be, part of us. This very close identification with us means that His miracle-potential is ours, too.

In spite of huge apathy, Jesus's love goes on pouring itself out. His heart stands ready to enter into all the pain of this earth in order to bring about life's one vital relationship: Jesus and us.

What a love we're watching with Mary! The sort of love which, in extreme agony, can notice that John and Mary, His own mother, will need to look after each other. The sort of love which means that the needs of you and me are constantly part of His awareness.

\* \* \*

Whenever we look at the Cross, we can make it *personal*.

In thinking about Jesus, as He hangs there, we may even "hear" Him speaking our name.

"John . . . Ann . . . Susan . . . David . . . this is for *you*."

## Changed By a Look

The amazing thing is that when we're conscious of having greatly failed Him, and hurt Him, the love of Jesus which we see on the Cross seems even stronger towards us. We just can't get over the extent of it. That's why we can never come away quite the same from a few minutes imaginatively spent watching the miracle of Jesus's love. So many of history's wonderfully changed lives start right here, just looking at that love. Right here, the Divine power starts to work in so many lives – even though, later, when miracles happen for us, we may forget just where it all started!

The heart of Jesus our Lord, feeling the pain of rejection in His creation, is deeply touched by every single response from one of His children when they think about the Cross. His gratitude for that response will open the door for marvellous things to happen in that person's life.

What we see happening at the Cross is the creation of a new situation in which miracles not only become possible but probable. Love won, and so we can begin to find hope about the very worst of our problems.

The link between that event two thousand years ago and present-day miracles is amazing. As hearts are melted by that love, huge barriers against the miraculous disappear, as if by magic. And the place which Jesus occupies in our hearts seems to get larger and larger!

If, every day, we can manage to think, for a few minutes, about that Cross, the miracle changes which we long to see in our lives are moving closer all the time. Strange that more people don't look back to that decisive event as the dynamic for miracles occurring in the twentieth century.

*       *       *

It looks as if we need to stay in Mary's company just a little longer, doesn't it? Otherwise, we won't be sharing with her what happened three days later!

Dear Lord,

I know the story so well. Help me to be very sure in my own heart that miracles flow from the love I'm looking at on the Cross. So that Your miracle-working power may not be obstructed in my own life, please let Your love sweep away all those occasions of hurting You – remembered or forgotten.

I allow no doubts about the greatness of Your love, and thank You now that in Your love I am forgiven.

Thank You that Your victory on the Cross is now shared with me, and that nothing is now impossible in my life.

# 12

# "Mary!"

Her eyes reddened by what must have been two days of almost continuous crying, Mary is still looking, hysterically, for some sign of her beloved Jesus. Love is overriding any considerations of tiredness, or of personal danger.

In Mary's empty world, even to see her Master in death might help just a little. But her conflict is tremendous.

Why had Jesus let them do it to Him, when they all needed Him so much?

Was Jesus mistaken?

Is God just a comforting thought that we've invented?

Dead people *stay* dead.

Even the appearance of an angelic being, outside an empty burial place, announcing that Jesus is alive again, is not enough for Mary in her tortured state. Even the memory of how her brother Lazarus had been restored to life by Jesus can be of little comfort now.

The "disappearance" of Jesus her Master seems like adding insult to the injury of His murder. All that Mary wants to do is to see Him. On top of everything else, Mary is now prevented from taking that final look; she can't give Jesus, perhaps, a last tender kiss. Mary has seen Jesus die but she is still, passionately,

His follower. Mary, in her heart, will never stop being His disciple.

\*    \*    \*

Having shared with the men disciples the empty-tomb experience, Mary now feels that she can't leave the garden, even though there's such a finality about cemeteries. The blackness for Mary is as deep as it can be. Almost certainly, Mary wouldn't mind dying herself, right now.

Then, in that garden, there's a moment which the greatest of romantic story-tellers could not have equalled.

"Mary!"

"Mary!" . . . A sound which must have echoed in her heart for weeks afterwards.

"Mary!" . . . The most beautiful single word spoken to anyone since the world began.

"Mary!" . . . Here is the miracle of Easter and, of course, the world hasn't been the same since.

The world certainly turns itself the right way up again for Mary, chosen for her Lord's first unmistakable appearance. Chosen because of her great need, and also, perhaps, because, in her heartbreak, she has never given up hope in Jesus.

And what about that moment in the garden for the risen Lord Himself? He must have been looking forward, so eagerly, to the oppportunity of giving Mary the happiest shock of her life. A very precious moment for both of them!

Easter has brought about for Mary, and for the world, one of those contrasts mentioned earlier – the darkness dramatically illuminated.

"I've seen the Lord", gasps Mary. Very soon others are saying, "Yes, so have we!"

All hell has been let loose in bringing about the rejection

and murder of Jesus; but how wonderfully God takes this opportunity to show that those who have trusted Him are right, after all.

It's as if there's a dazzling light shining around the Cross, around the Easter garden, and, from now on, around the lives of all who follow Jesus.

## Love's Continuance

Over the next six weeks we know that Jesus makes a number of brief "appearances". Peter apparently has one all to himself – he needed it! Two disciples on a country road, with Jesus on their minds, have a brief but convincing glimpse of Him. And then, dear old cautious Thomas seems to have caused Jesus to reappear one evening just for him.

It's interesting that Paul, writing about thirty years later, mentions Jesus appearing to about five hundred people, most of them still alive at the time of writing. It could well have been a sort of "farewell reunion" for His many friends, and the people He had helped! Then, of course, there was that very special breakfast on the shore . . .

The appearances are brief – but compelling. Jesus's friends have become as sure of Him when they can't see Him as when they could.

It's as if they now see not only the sharp and painful contrast of living and dying, but something of the Divine perspective, in which death on this finite planet is almost irrelevant compared with the fact of God and the continuance of His love.

Somehow, the disciples' hope in Jesus's person had never died, in spite of the hard facts of the crucifixion.

This makes them ready for the very first signs of their Lord's continued existence. But "ready" does not exactly mean expecting! It seems pretty clear that most of the disciples are *not* expecting what happens. In other words, the appearances of Jesus our Lord are not "wish-fulfilling" illusions.

These are cautious, even sceptical, people whose scepticism can only be blasted away by something wonderful happening. Although people still argue about what exactly the disciples "see" on their various meetings with Jesus over six weeks, it's almost a historical certainty that they themselves are absolutely convinced. They can't argue about the atomic reconstruction of the resurrection-body, or any of the other issues which people have debated. They just *know*.

## Logical

As Jesus returns, to shock both the sentimental and the hard-headed ones into believing, it's the great demonstration that the material world, despite appearances, is not all that there is. It is the great demonstration that at the heart of this puzzling creation, there is love. It is the best piece of news that the world has ever received.

Soon hundreds of men and women followers of Jesus are radiantly and infectiously happy, ready to look emperors in the face and to die, if necessary, rather than deny what they have experienced. Jesus's friends are like football supporters coming away from a match, grabbing the first person who has not heard the result, and saying, "We won . . . we won!"

Most of these people have been eye-witnesses of the miracles before the crucifixion. Now, they have seen the world-changing miracle of their beloved Lord back from the dead. It is as if, after helping so many individuals in need, Jesus has come back on Easter morning to say to the rest of us: "Now *this* one is for *all* of you!"

\*   \*   \*

The victory of Jesus our Lord did not, of course, provide a convincing "proof" to satisfy everyone in the centuries which followed. What that victory did in a still dark world was to give some light to each person prepared to trust in God's existence. Our Lord's words to Thomas about believing without seeing were meant for us, of course.

So often we speculate, wistfully, about whether there's an afterlife. There are believers who have the gravest doubts about this and feel they daren't indulge in the luxury of that comforting thought.

But, because God exists . . .

the rising of Jesus from the dead is logical;
the miracles of Jesus (of all kinds) are logical;
our continued existence after this life is logical.

This is why I believe most strongly, for example, that our loved ones who have died really will be waiting to welcome us in that other sphere of existence, and that we'll have a face-to-face meeting with Jesus!

I realize that a phrase like "the miracle of Easter" can slip easily off the pen. But it was a miracle, wasn't it? A decisive breakthrough by the supernatural dimension into the material world, so that a young man, well and truly dead and carted off for burial, is back, two days later, to transform His friends. No matter how it happened, it happened. And people find support for their belief in the resurrection-miracle by what they experience of Jesus now!

And so we really have got something to look forward to, rather than the eventual extinction of our solar system. But, of course, what happened to Jesus gives us so much more than hope, doesn't it? That victory makes miracle-power available for us in the sophisticated but harsh world of the late twentieth century.

\* \* \*

Well, here are Jesus's friends after that Easter morning. They're increasingly certain that anything in life which might make them afraid is now powerless to harm them. Soon they are "power-full" people, who change history.

The age of miracles hasn't been cruelly cut short by the crucifixion, after all. It is only beginning.

---

Dear Lord,

When things are slow to change, when doubts about You creep in, I will respond by thinking, immediately, of Your Easter victory.

I will anticipate the victory which there is going to be in my own life, simply because I've put my hope in You.

Lord, I believe that any darkness for us in this life is only temporary. I believe that the light which started to shine again at Easter will one day illuminate everything – and everyone!

---

# 13

# A Hard Act To Follow!

There's a vital period linking Jesus's Palestine miracles
and those which He performs for so many of us today.
People don't always study this period very thoroughly,
but it's well worth doing so. Not only is it exciting, but it
gives us lots of clues about how God's power works
through ordinary people.

This crucial period is, of course, the one in which our
Lord's followers moved about the Mediterranean world,
without His physical presence, but doing some amazing
things. At first, those disciples would feel completely
inadequate – as someone said, Jesus was a very difficult
act to follow. He had concluded an incredible three years
by rising from the dead. How could they compete with
that?

\*　　\*　　\*

Some of the little group had, of course, already experienced "going it alone" when Jesus sent them out as
missionaries, returning excitedly to report healings, and
the removal of evil spirits. Then, when about to leave
them, we know that He made it crystal-clear that this
work was to continue. All that the apostles had to do,
now, was to use the power which would be transferred to

them. "You'll be able to put your hands on sick people, and they'll get better", Jesus told them.

Well, that's all very fine when Jesus is with you. But soon all they had was a memory. The disciples had seen Jesus in action and it had taught them a lot. But they had no manuals, no "keys to working a miracle", no "How to" books (I realize the danger when writing this!) They just had . . . a promise.

Those followers of Jesus were so like us, weren't they? We find personal weaknesses, guilt feelings, a tendency to be discouraged, even instances of one or two touchy relationships among them. Well, that's encouraging for a start! And so how did those apostles go on to do such amazing things? Among the more obvious reasons was their belief that in the hostile world they were now facing, Jesus still existed. Most had seen Him after the resurrection. But there's another and *tremendously important reason*. There was a burning desire for Jesus their Lord to show up well. They were not interested in fame or "fulfilment" for themselves, they just wanted people to know how wonderful was their Jesus. And this was crucial. Jesus to show up well in an indifferent world – that's what His followers wanted. And that's exactly what Jesus obligingly did for them!

Another reason for the miracles which occurred in the very early Church was that these men and women realized that in everything, it was God, not them. No professional "expertise", and basking in it! The apostles were soon aware that the risen Jesus did not do things in response to any arm-twisting by them, but only as He chose. Those were normal people, prepared for abnormal things to be done by Jesus through them. And so, off they went.

It's worth pausing, isn't it, to look at what those apostles had, as we try to serve Jesus today? They had:

## God's Opportunities

1. A certainty about the Divine power working through Jesus.
2. A desire for Him to look good – rather than themselves.
3. A realization that it all depended on Him.

Sometimes, today, these get a little obscured!

## The Explosion

Well, we know that for Jesus's followers it was not a sort of "spiritual bliss" existence, the sort of thing we read about in one or two of those "Cloud 7" books today. We know that those apostles had to endure much suffering; they were far from universally loved; they were a threat to the Establishment; they were people in danger. But whenever those early Christians came into a new town or village it wasn't long before things started happening!

The explosion which really had got things moving, of course, was God delegating His power on the Day of Pentecost. Those friends of Jesus had had at least a month's wait! Some could have become distinctly uneasy, perhaps doubtful. Then . . . Well, we know the story, don't we?

It was as if everything which Jesus had won for us was suddenly made available. The fire of God falls, and immediately people are on fire for God. Here are the languages needed to spread the Good News around the Mediterranean; an intoxicating happiness – for everyone to see. Intoxicating! Yes, we can't escape the sceptics for very long. "These Jesus-people have had a little too much liquid refreshment!" But Peter, bless him, makes the very practical point: "The pubs aren't open yet."

The sceptics were looking for any "explanation" other than the one that God was doing something. But soon Jerusalem is buzzing with the news. "Hey! Have you heard what happened to old Simon?" (He was the beggar at the Temple gate.) God was seen at work, and as Paul said later, "Our message hasn't been based on eloquence, but on a demonstration of God's power."

\* \* \*

Yes, in spite of all the human limitations of Jesus's followers, the power flows. We watch Peter and John on that routine (or was it?) visit to the Temple.

Old Simon at the gate isn't going to let Peter and John go past without a hand-out if he can help it. "We don't have any money", says Peter. Then, prompted by God to respond to this opportunity, Peter takes Simon by the hand and says, "In the name of Jesus – walk!" Simon scrambles to his feet immediately and, after a pause, starts walking. Then – and this is quite a common sight after Jesus has taken an opportunity – Simon does more than walk: he leaps. As the liberated Simon praises and dances around, the large crowd are tremendously impressed. Peter is quick to explain – "This is not because of *our* spirituality."

We're not sure why we don't hear very much, in the days which follow, of some of the more prominent disciples. We gradually hear less and less of Peter. Poor John fades right out, though he does crop up later as a writer! But soon upon the scene comes a man who is to make the greatest impact of them all . . .

Dear Lord,

As I read about the young Church I realize, more and more, that it was far from easy for them. Thank You for the encouragement of knowing that weak people, very likely to fail You at any time, could still do wonderful things in Your strength.

# 14

# Why The Power Flowed

Soon to be completely overwhelmed by the continued flow of God's power is that arch-enemy of the Jesus-people, our friend Saul! With the burning fixation that the dangerous Jesus cult must be stopped, Saul looks as if he might even succeed . . . until . . .

Until he is stopped dead in his tracks. Saul hears the voice of Jesus, "Why are you persecuting Me, Saul?" Jesus is starting to work on a most unlikely candidate for the ministry!

Without going into the dramatic sequence, we simply note that the blinded Saul is helped into nearby Damascus. In a lovely moment, Ananias, one of the new believers, obeys a Divine prompting . . . and there's a miracle. Saul gets back his sight, and is now that human dynamo for Jesus, Paul.

As we look at this recruitment of Paul, we see God taking the most unpromising opportunity, as He so often does today. Working on absolutely nothing, except His knowledge of Paul's potential, God gets Himself an ambassador-extraordinary.

Back to Peter. In Lydda, Peter meets Aeneas, so badly paralysed that he has spent the past eight years in bed. "Aeneas," says Peter, "I want you to know that Jesus has healed you. You can get up out of that bed." And Aeneas does. No wonder the entire population is reported to have become converts.

Here we are in Joppa, by the blue "Med". Peter is confronted, as his Master had been, with the ultimate challenge.

Dorcas, a real light in that little Christian community, has died, her body laid out in an upstairs room ready for burial. What makes two of Dorcas's friends send a message to Peter in nearby Lydda we shall never know, but they're about to become partners in the taking of a Divine opportunity. Peter arrives to find a room full of Dorcas's weeping friends. Asking the mourners to leave, Peter kneels and prays. Looking at the body, "Get up, Dorcas", he says. Dorcas opens her eyes and sits up, and Peter presents her alive to the others. The news about Dorcas was quick to spread, and there don't seem to have been many unbelievers in Joppa at that time.

\* \* \*

Paul, after his amazing turn-round, finds himself literally surrounded by opportunities for the power of God to be demonstrated. At Lystra, Paul tells a man crippled from birth to stand up. No need to say what happened! It is important to notice that Paul and Barnabas stress that *they* must not be hero-worshipped. It was God who was doing the miracles, as Peter had pointed out.

In Philippi, Paul has to confront an evil entity which is ruining the life of a slave-girl. "I command you, in the name of Jesus, to come out", says Paul . . . and it does.

The miracles in this exciting period are varied. Here are Paul and Silas in prison. (Yes, it is hazardous, then, to be a Jesus-person.) But the doors fly open, and chains fall off the prisoners. The poor jailer thinks of suicide, rather than face what's coming. But Paul says, "Now, there's no need to do anything to yourself. We're all here!" We note the jailer's wonderful request – "Sirs, what must I do to be saved?" And the equally wonderful, economical reply: "Believe in Jesus – and you will be!" A God who can release His friends from prison so effortlessly is worth enquiring about, and so the jailer and his family become believers, joyful ones!

It is inevitable that Paul, like Peter, will come across the challenge of death itself. The tragedy this time is caused by that long sermon. Falling asleep during Paul's address, a young man falls to his death from an upstairs window. Paul goes down and puts his arm around the dead man, who is restored to life. It's conjecture whether Paul then pressed on to make point Number Six or not!

All sorts of eye-opening things occur as God takes His opportunities in Malta, Turkey, Greece . . .

Particularly exciting are occasions where the apostles are involved in multiple healings.

There are a number of references to groups of people finding miraculous healing on certain occasions, just as had happened when Jesus was besieged by sick people.

## *The Power-Base*

As we look carefully at the early Church in action, we begin to see that there is a key which unlocks doors. That key is, of course, the unique power of Jesus. When that power is (1) believed in and (2) used, the supernatural dimension breaks into material conditions and changes them.

Those early Christians were focused on Jesus their Lord, and so people in need found a vital point of contact with the supernatural, from which the power flowed.

Paul, Peter and the others had simply made themselves completely "available" to God – who could use them wherever they went. Luke, writing his gospel and then continuing in his Acts of the Apostles, obviously sees (1) Jesus and (2) His followers doing the same miracle work.

On those journeys to spread the Good News, all sorts of barriers were removed, and no personal discouragements affected the power-flow. People's natural resistance crumbled, as they responded, as they always will, to acts of compassion and power. It was all due to the risen Jesus's presence.

Miracles kept happening because His followers never let Jesus become divorced from them as their power-base. They lived with a Jesus-consciousness. So many "ways of service" and "special efforts" in the Church today are only partially effective, because there is not this uncompromising Jesus-awareness, and total reliance on Him.

Wasn't Paul a marvellous example for us? So often lonely, so often misunderstood, Paul never lost the will to bring God's love to people. Like us, Paul was painfully aware of (and so *frank* about) shortcomings. But Paul managed to discipline his interior life so that the one thing which mattered – the flow of Jesus's power to change people's lives – could continue. Paul was never anything less than obsessed with his beloved Jesus. Miracle-opportunities simply followed!

Although much of the apostles' lives, like ours, must have been routine and unspectacular, their love of Jesus meant that humdrum situations kept being lit up by God's wonders. Just as they are today.

Lord,

Never let me forget that You choose to work through fallible people . . . who simply look to You for what is needed.

Let me be one who helps to recapture, in the twentieth century, the victorious spirit, and the sheer love, of those early followers of Yours.

Thank You

# 15

# Wonders Have Never Ceased

It's amazing how some of the things which Christians wrote about in the first few centuries have been virtually ignored!

We can read of people miraculously restored to health, men and women returning to sanity after being prayed for, and miracles, generally, being taken for granted. Gradually the miracles became more spaced out. One reason for this, I'm sure, was that the Church became increasingly formal and less adventurous!

In spite of the Church's growing orthodoxy and "respectability", however, healing miracles kept popping up, and occasions of tremendous joy are recorded as Jesus seems to have just overwhelmed His followers with a sense of His presence.

Justin Martyr, in the second century, quotes some spectacular examples of people being freed from illness and possession. Irenaeus, Bishop of Lyons, shows clearly that it was quite normal for Christians to lay their hands on sick people and to see a recovery made. There were exorcisms, visions, and inspired prophecies.

Tertullian, in one of his fluent descriptions, actually gives names of people who had been made well, and liberated, when prayed for. Later writers, such as Jerome, and the great Augustine, continue the story.

Augustine in *The City of God* listed many miracles, and expressed regret that there were a lot of others which he hadn't space to mention.

It's clear that among people with love for Jesus, miracles have always been happening. The healing powers of St Francis in the medieval era were well known. Because of the very sane and detailed accounts of lives like those of Francis and Augustine we have a strong sense of God always at work through the centuries.

\*     \*     \*

It's only today that almost everyone feels that they must write a book (sorry!) It wasn't always so, and the rather few records we have of miraculous happenings through the centuries obviously cover only a tiny fraction of God's activity.

In days when existence was harder for most than it is now, it is clear that God took countless opportunities to bring light into people's lives. Experiences of power, and of sheer happiness, were seen in the lives of John Wesley, and of so many others, reaching into the present day.

It has always been a minority, of course, who have lived very close to God, rather than being just "formal" Christians. The things which that minority have had to report have always been exciting. And it's certain that, quite apart from what He has done in the lives of that devout minority, God has always been active over a much wider area. This, of course, is because of His sheer love for all His children in need, even the "indifferent" ones.

There seems to be a definite pattern to the way in which God has dealt with His world through the centuries. He has, first of all, led so many of His children to recognize their need; then, there has been recognition of Him through the meeting of those needs; those people became people who *knew* . . . and were able to reach out lovingly to their contemporaries, who were still puzzled about life.

And so, God's love-activity in drawing people to know and trust Him has just gone steadily on, cutting right across things like temperament and environment. The sad part is that loss of expectancy which, in so many lives, has restricted that activity.

Joyful things have kept happening in the lives of Christians who have retained that sense of expectancy, and who have seen God providing for them, and protecting them, in marvellous ways. In every age, wherever the Lord Jesus Christ has been trusted, and lovingly worshipped, there has been this constant Divine opportunity-taking. Wonders have never ceased.

## Miracles on Our Hands

What seems to be happening in the second half of the twentieth century? Well, it's certain that more and more people are finding that exciting faith which we spoke about at the start, a faith which expects and really sees miracles. It's as if there is a sharper focusing of the creative, healing energies of God for specific needs, as increasing numbers now pray expectantly.

When sceptics are always ready to rush in with "natural" explanations, we have to be a little cautious about labelling something a "miracle". Or do we? There's no doubt at all in my mind that where Jesus is loved and trusted there's a distinct release of power, and we find ourselves, so often, with a miracle on our hands!

As we start to accept that God is deeply involved and

active in His world, with His influence upon every detail, we find ourselves amazed by the way in which He does things.

\*     \*     \*

There's a joyous character from the U.S.A., Pastor John Wimber, who has been a channel of God's healing all over the world and who has seen many dramatic and remarkable things. His verdict: "Today there are more people praying for miracles, and miracles *happening*, than for a very long time."

Father Michael Scanlon, who has seen many emotional problems disappear through prayer, always writes with great care not to claim as miracles, things which are not. Nevertheless Father Scanlon says: "We have heard people cry out in agony and emotional turmoil, and heard them later sing out in peace and freedom. We have seen men and women bound with chains of despair and self-hatred later appear as lights of hope . . . loving themselves, and others."

It really does seem that, if we're ready to accept that God has never stopped working miracles, He's going to let us see lots of them in the twentieth century! A young man known to me was prayed for, some years ago, for a growth on his tongue which had caused him, among other things, to lose his voice. A frightening situation. The growth, however, just disappeared when prayer was concentrated upon it, and when the doctor saw what had happened, he almost fell off his chair. You can look at the case notes to this day and see the entry: "A healing which I can only put down to Divine intervention."

However, I've not forgotten my promise that we shall not be looking, mainly, at spectacular miracles like the one just mentioned. We'll be looking, instead, at those frequent, quieter, but still miraculous, examples of God's opportunity-taking. I'm sure we're going to notice these instances increasingly, and find ourselves changing because of them.

---

Dear Lord,

Thank You for responding, in love, to people's needs through the centuries. Thank You for all that You are doing today. In spite of occasional exaggerations, and false claims, I thank You for the countless genuine miracle-changes in people's lives. If I have to wait a little longer for *my* miracle, please don't let my disappointment turn to scepticism. I'll keep looking in Your direction expectantly . . . knowing that I *will* become someone in whose life You have taken yet another opportunity.

Thank You

---

# 16

# Crisis-Encounters

Before we do at last get down to preparing for some miracles in our own lives, could we take just a peep into the world of hospitals today?

Hospitals, of course, are places where there are many prayers being said all the time, very hesitant and only half-believing prayers, as well as prayers full of radiant faith! It's not surprising, therefore, that there are an awful lot of really happy experiences, and changed lives, in spite of the wan faces and tears.

I've seen Jesus our Lord taking opportunities in countless dark situations. I've seen Him reveal Himself to people in ways which never cease to amaze me. It's as if He is forcing a number of those unhappy circumstances to have some good result. He does it all so beautifully, and so often it is in ways which we could not have anticipated. There isn't always physical healing for patients, of course, but the transforming power of Jesus can be seen in so many instances. Relatives and friends often find themselves saying things like, "Whatever *happened* to our John while he was in hospital?"

\* \* \*

Brian was rushed into hospital after attempting suicide. He had been caught out after a series of systematic frauds in his job, and almost all the money obtained from these frauds had been squandered on generally "living it up". Brian knew that there were hardly any extenuating circumstances, and that he was likely to lose his wife and little girl because of it all. So he decided to take his own life. Only a neighbour's prompt intervention ensured that Brian did not die.

The one ray of hope in the situation was that Brian started coming to the little church in the hospital and began to look for God in the midst of the mess he was in. I feared that, with a court appearance ahead, and a broken marriage, Brian might again attempt suicide when leaving the security of the hospital.

Well, Brian really threw everything into securing God's help, and even when going on weekend leave from the hospital, would make the considerable journey to be at the hospital's morning service.

I knew that Brian was praying hard, as the day for his appearance in court drew close – and so of course was I! The court was told that Brian's marriage was, in fact, at an end. And then a stiff sentence was passed. Very composed, but with tears in his eyes, Brian faced a dark future. Soon afterwards, in prison, Brian was told that his little girl of six was having all sorts of problems, including nightmares, in the absence of the Daddy she loved.

But it hadn't been a wasted exercise to bring in Jesus. From prison, Brian wrote about the sense of peace which his prayers and his reading of the Bible were giving to him. Soon, there was talk of his early release. Then, on a momentous visiting day, Brian and his wife, Shirley, decided that they would stay together, in spite of everything.

Soon Brian wrote that his prison sentence was over,

and could he and Shirley come to the little hospital church for a blessing of their marriage – a completely new start?

I don't think I've ever enjoyed going through a marriage service more than this one. No one else was there, just the three of us. Over a cup of coffee, Brian revealed that the idea of the little ceremony had been Shirley's. Then Brian said this:

"I'm glad that we asked God to do this today, because He's been in it all along!" Yes, a terribly messed-up situation had been (you've guessed it) another opportunity for Jesus our Lord.

\* \* \*

Hospital wards, in spite of all the sadness around you, are natural settings for miracles. The people I've met are certainly worth another book in itself.

You can see so many people simply "becoming believers", God giving them a trust which they don't lose when the crisis is over. You can see families who have been deadly enemies for years tearfully embracing each other at bedsides. You hear, many times, of things like visions, and uncanny experiences of God's warm presence, and these usually from "sensible" people! You see the miracle of those with terrible afflictions and handicaps finding that they have the gift of lifting the spirits of other people in the ward.

In hospitals you're very conscious of God reaching into the deeply hurt places of so many people and giving them, at this crisis time, a sense of how much He loves them. You see people starting to be "kind to themselves" instead of punishing themselves; you see people start expecting good things to happen, instead of dreading what the next few hours may bring.

\* \* \*

I must admit that in hospitals, and in other crisis settings, it does seem a little easier to do the sort of thing which is the subject of our book: recognizing God at work. In a crisis setting there seems to be, so often, a heightened awareness of God's presence, of Him giving surprising courage, of Him supporting and protecting.

An obvious reason for the awareness, of course, is that so many of the illusions, and false supports, are no longer there, and people come face to face with themselves. And because God longs to bring someone home to Himself at any stage of life, He's more than ready to take the opportunity of the faintest "enquiry", in someone's mind, about Him.

This awakening of a sense of need is happening all the time, of course. Reaching out to God, so many find real and lasting change such as a temporarily "manufactured" God could never have supplied for them. The crisis time signalled the start of miracle work. There must be hundreds and thousands of people – firm believers now – who first learned the art of seeing God at work during a stay in hospital.

\*   \*   \*

I've stopped being surprised at the number of those walking-miracles who had come into hospital full of despair, but who later (even with physical problems still there) beamed at me and said something like: "I'm glad I had to come in here because God has come to mean something at last."

In hospitals you do, of course, find much bitterness. You also see people with their defences down, complaining, or very scared. But you see, so often, the miracle of people being brought by Jesus (using hospital as a unique opportunity) into a special relationship with Himself.

The things which happen in these wards have convinced me that, as we said at the start, the human race, itself, is a miracle. You see the qualities of compassion, courage, extreme patience, hope, and quiet joy, all when circumstances are as "unfavourable" as they could possibly be.

It all makes you even more sure about Jesus – who started the whole process!

---

Dear Lord,

Thank You for the overpowering miracles . . . but thank You, especially, at this time, for the quiet ones – such as those which are always happening in hospitals.

Give me the capacity to see the miraculous in the events of each day . . . I don't have to go into hospital to do this! And, Lord, I do believe in Your power to put right all sorts of things in my life . . . so that I really do become a new person.

Thank You

---

# 17

# Seeing God At Work

I hope that after "watching" Jesus perform those miracles, the habit of seeing Him at work might continue!

As we have looked at the difference which Jesus made in people's lives I know that He will have been working in us. And so, if we're even just a little more expectant now about present-day miracles, there is every reason to be!

It's tempting to say that the Palestine episode was exceptional, and that we can't remotely expect such things to happen today. Well, yes, there is a big difference, obviously. In Palestine, the veil between the spiritual and material dimensions was lifted sufficiently for people to be literally overwhelmed by the sight of God at work. But it's also true that God doesn't change! The situations which Jesus confronted on earth, of course, were just like those of today, and the Divine power is the same. Above all, the love He has for us is the same, and the risen Jesus Christ now has a much wider sphere in which to work. We could even say that we have one advantage over the thousands in Palestine who never got near to Him, in that any one of us now has access to Him.

Having said that, I do have to admit that this accessibility would be so much helped if we had His physical presence! Jesus our Lord knew that there would be this problem when He spoke about those who could not see Him but still managed to believe.

But the presence of Jesus does become increasingly real for us as we let Him share life with us, and as we bring our needs to Him. We become conscious of the love which prompted His miracles. The countless interventions in the present day to change a "natural" course of events (which would often be catastrophic for us), are simply a continuation of that loving activity.

\*  \*  \*

It's worth taking a deep breath as we think of some of the often neglected things which have naturally miraculous consequences. The deep breath is to make sure that although we're aware of some urgent current needs, our ideas are not too rigid about what we would like God to do for us. As you know, false hopes can so easily be raised when a person thinks, "If God can do something about this arthritis (or my marriage) I'll certainly believe in miracles."

Over-expectancy about the kind of things God will do, or about their timing, can, of course, lead to disappointments. Nevertheless, I'm sure that we shall now experience, increasingly, the joy of seeing those miraculous interventions of each day!

For many of us, our expectancy will be struggling to survive in the midst of extremely difficult, even frightening, present circumstances. That is why my prayer for each one of us reading this has been that the presence of Jesus would be realized more than ever, bringing changes which are independent of basic temperament, or of personal circumstances.

# God's Opportunities
## Natural

Many things are attempted in the hope of obtaining miracles! It could be our slipping, self-consciously, into that crowded festival of praise and healing. It could be a solitary reaching out to God, in sheer panic.

Were we disappointed, perhaps, after that charismatic personality, full of faith, had prayed for us, and yet we felt (and still feel) no different? Well, it's worth remembering that God so often does things in response to our *gentle* pressures, not necessarily responding to heightened faith-charged atmosphere, but to the almost undetectable. (I'm not forgetting, by the way, Bartimaeus and Co., whose approach to Jesus wasn't exactly undetectable!)

As we grow closer to Jesus our scarcely detectable longings bring, in a natural way, some marvellous responses. I could mention, straightaway, four things from which Divine interventions in our lives naturally flow. Here they are:

1. A really *big* view of Jesus (explained shortly).
2. Opening up *all* our life to Him (with no limiting factors, such as, "Just my insomnia, please, Lord").
3. Giving Him plenty of our attention (an "awareness" of Jesus usually carries with it, too, an awareness of His working).
4. That sense of expectancy – which can even accept situations becoming temporarily worse, knowing that Jesus will not fail to answer our prayers.

We'll look later at some other things with a miracle-potential which we can learn to make habitual.

It is hard to put out of our mind some very urgent

need, but it's better if we can, as far as possible, make our focus Jesus Himself. There are always certain natural consequences of that focusing, truly miraculous, without straining to see that specific miracle in our life. Seeing Jesus a little better, means a growing recognition of His work for us.

## *Extravagant*

Shall we look at that "big" view of Jesus?

There used to be characters who stood outside racetracks and football grounds, carrying banners with the challenging question "What Think Ye of Christ?" Sometimes, on the other side of the banner (causing you to hurry into the soccer game, feeling slightly uneasy) was: "Prepare to Meet Thy Doom!"

But that first question, "What do we really think of Jesus?", is so important, that it would be lovely if we could settle it right now.

There has always been controversy about the person of Jesus, especially among thoughtful agnostics and, of course, among theologians. Sometimes Jesus is the dynamic risen Lord, busy on our behalf every day; sometimes He's a slightly enigmatic figure from the past, who just might have been a little mistaken about His supernatural origins.

I always find it incredible that people who manage a belief in the supernatural can nevertheless have such wishy-washy views about Jesus.

The big intellectual hurdle in this life is whether or not God is there at all. When we're over that hurdle, and feel pretty confident that we are believers, then I feel that the way is open to accept everything which surrounds Jesus.

We can be *thrilled* at His words, "If you've seen Me, you've seen God the Father". We can be *thrilled* at all those miracles.

I believe that there's a stage in our lives when (in spite of one or two intellectual difficulties on the subject) Jesus somehow "lights up" for us. We feel that if we have Jesus, there's nothing else we need. If we're not relying too much on our limited reasoning powers, God's Spirit can seem to whisper inside us, "Jesus . . . now there's someone who can be absolutely everything for you."

I'm not saying, of course, that it all rests on some sort of "correct" belief, in a narrow or fanatical sense. Sometimes, in people like that, the sheer love of Jesus isn't reflected at all. But I've found that there's an absolutely vital link between a "big" view (a really extravagant view!) of Jesus, and . . . miracles.

If someone believes the very best of us, it does help us to go into action on behalf of that person, doesn't it? Jesus our Lord is surely no different.

Obviously, Jesus doesn't need that "big" view of Him in order to intervene majestically (He has often performed miracles for people who thought they were atheists), but through the centuries we find this link between an extravagant view of Jesus and miraculous happenings.

For these early apostles, "Jesus is Lord" was enough. God was the Person they could see in Jesus. Jesus was *the answer* for them, and what He did through those apostles proved it.

If Jesus becomes, even slightly, a shadowy figure, who may or may not have done the things reported, how can we honestly expect very much to happen? Marvellous things occur when there is this child-like, extravagant concept of Jesus. In our hearts, I know that each one of us would love to think we were in this category. If we want to be, He'll help us to be!

"Tell us, Jesus," said some of His disciples, "what can *we* do to make miracles happen?"

There was a memorable and decisive answer: "If you want to see miracles, then believe in God's Son . . . the One who's with you now."

"Believe in" – a single-minded and absolutely trusting attitude towards the Person of Jesus.

## Caring Control

I have said that there are many helpful conditions in which miracles seem to occur, but it's worth getting this one, about our "big" view of Jesus, settled once and for all, don't you think?

It's such a *relaxing* thing when we've settled that

(1) Jesus really is supreme in creation, and
(2) Jesus has first place in our own life (this can be a little harder than number one!)

Yes, relaxing . . . in the staggering thought that Jesus, as we said earlier, actually brought us into being. Has this *really* got hold of us?

Relaxing . . . in the knowledge that the influence of the risen Jesus is all around us, that we cannot go anywhere (even if some sort of galaxy-jump is perfected) which is out of His care.

Relaxing . . . in the knowledge that Jesus can't isolate Himself from our experiences, and that all we could possibly need for getting through this life can be found in Him.

Relaxing . . . in His own description of Himself as "Friend" (i.e. *wanting* our happiness).

Relaxing . . . in the certainty that Jesus is in loving
control of every detail of the situation we are in right
now, and waiting for the opportunity to bring about the
best possible answers to our prayers.

Incidentally, a nice, unhurried private decision to be a
"child-like" and expectant person, as far as Jesus is concerned, can be tremendously helpful here. After such a
decision it is never too long before we see things
happening which point to Him – and, coupled with this,
a sense of His nearness.

I always feel that it is a good idea for anyone, however
long a Christian, to settle quietly, in Jesus's presence, the
matter of His supremacy. There's a suggested prayer at
the end of the chapter, but our own words are usually
best!

I'm sure that allowing ourselves to have this uncompromising and extravagant view of Jesus will be more
than enough, before reading on, to ensure that miracles
are on the way!

### Inter-woven

It wasn't only the miracle work of Jesus which was
absolutely bang-on, of course. So was His advice to us!
And what He said was this: Be like a branch which
doesn't get itself severed from the main tree. In other
words, combining that "big" view of Jesus with keeping
close.

I realize that all this may sound rather obvious, but
how much these vital things can be neglected by
thousands of "disappointed" Christians. For the
closeness to operate we need to make sure that a
wholehearted opportunity for Jesus's involvement has

been deliberately given, that we've opened up ourselves, and all our future, to the source of our life.

Watching for God to take opportunities is obviously so much better if our life is like a house which doesn't have to be broken into. This complete opening of the door of one's life has often been left out by many churchgoing people, who now feel that they're missing something. He doesn't want to do only a partial job in us. Even if we still have problem areas, the involvement means an extension of God's area of influence, and miraculous changes must follow . . . some soon, some eventually.

Yes, Jesus wants His life to be inter-woven with our own. We'll find ourselves forgiving more easily, rising above circumstances, praying lovingly . . . all miracle-producing conditions!

The incredible changes in people, of the sort which amaze onlookers, are not due to methods, powerful "suggestion", self-improvement programmes, stage-managed miracles, or the temporary manufacturing of a sort of spiritual intensity. These changes are a natural and automatic result of a close relationship with mankind's Friend.

Where there is this close relationship, we can take for granted that He is intervening in ways which He sees as good for us, now, and in the long term.

Keeping close to Jesus and being completely open to His influence, are not unrealizable platitudes. We begin to share with our Lord an environment in which we increasingly detect His work. It's an environment in which we really enjoy Jesus leading us – because we want to have such a wonderful person in charge!

Lord Jesus,

May it be the base on which the rest of my life is built that You are in control of all things.

May I worship You as God, and trust You, with no reservations.

Lord, I *decide*, right now, to be an expectant person . . . believing the very best of You.

Thank You, Lord Jesus Christ, that You are supreme in creation. May You always be in first place, too, in my own heart.

Thank You for the opportunities You will now be taking in my life, as we become increasingly involved with each other. With You, I know that all things are now possible for me.

Thank You again

# 18

# The Miracle-Name

I wonder if we could put something into practice straight-away, assuming that we're not already doing so?

There is a word spoken, even in semi-belief, or with very little real hope, which can change situations in a truly miraculous way. This miracle-producing word has been spoken in extreme pain; spoken in the devastation of losing a loved one; spoken when all one's dreams have collapsed; spoken when faith has become almost non-existent; spoken in threatening circumstances of so many kinds.

You will know, of course, what that word is!

\*　　\*　　\*

The Name JESUS, barely whispered, perhaps, in a fear situation, or when the world is suddenly cold and empty, proves to be of tremendous power.

Said at any time, it brings the supernatural and its influence into the foreground. "Jesus" . . . and the door is opened for the kind of help which no one else can give to us.

\*　　\*　　\*

It's not always realized that Jesus our Lord has lent us His Name to be *used*. Even if said mechanically, or a little self- consciously, it injects a new factor into a situation. The speaking of Jesus's Name, either to ourselves or to Him, is not a sort of magic formula which works with a few suggestible people. The barely audible use of our Lord's Name, in fact, acts as a remover of barriers. There are times when even the briefest prayer seems beyond us, and rational thinking has stopped completely. At such times, with what little effort we may have left in us, the Miracle-Name can be quietly used. Using that Name, although we may not be fully aware of it at the time, means the start of miraculous intervention in our situation.

\*   \*   \*

**Jesus** . . . indicating that only He can make a real difference at this moment.

**Jesus** . . . showing that trust, though very fragile, is still there.

**Jesus** . . . and a sense of belonging begins to return.

**Jesus** . . . and influences of a kind which could worsen my situation are firmly checked.

**Jesus** . . . and the power underlying all creation is being channelled for my very specific need of this moment.

**Jesus** . . . and the resources built up during past prayerful contacts with Him are now being drawn upon.

**Jesus** . . . and the growing sense of being part of the Person whose Name I'm speaking.

**Jesus** . . . and a realization that because of His love, His purposes for me are not going to be deflected by anything that is happening now.

**Jesus** . . . and the wounding-power of any present circumstances is inter-penetrated by something else – that first intimation of His peace.

**Jesus** . . . and I'm aware that the circumstances of this moment are being used as part of that drawing closer to Himself which He has promised.

**Jesus** . . . and the growing sense that although I may be feeling defeated right now, He is not.

**Jesus** . . . and I remember how wonderfully He has already brought me through so many threatening situations.

**Jesus** . . . the realization that He knew my present circumstances were coming – and has prepared precisely what I need in them.

\*　　\*　　\*

The saying of Jesus's Name will soon become instinctive, whether said confidently or helplessly. It is a Miracle-Name because Jesus our Lord is the one relevant factor for change in any human situation.

Lord Jesus,

Every time my thoughts turn to You, every time I whisper Your Name, I can be sure of Your presence – and Your influence.

Your influence, and my awareness of You, however faint, will be crucial in any temporary darkness, or pressure of external circumstances, which may exist.

Your influence will create the conditions for peace and hope to be felt, when, from the world's point of view, they should not be.

Thank You for giving Your Name to be used. I will certainly use it now.

The things we are looking at in our book will make God's miracle-interventions more real to us, but let's still keep in mind that they are not a cold-blooded "making of the right conditions" which force Him to act!

The important thing to remember is that an increased miracle-potential in our lives is the natural and inevitable result of that relationship.

Well, here are just a few aspects of the relationship:

"Bringing Jesus into" every situation, until it becomes instinctive.

That really large view of Jesus . . . miracles resulting from our decision to put Him on a pedestal!

Those first hesitant steps of "trying out" the power of Jesus against negative influences, and finding that it works.

Learning to look away from problem areas, and towards Jesus. Not just for crisis times, but a look which is habitual, through each day, so that we do not miss so much of what He's doing!

Letting an awareness of Jesus's love become a more or less constant thing.

Learning the art of forgiving and being forgiven.

Switching off the world for a time during a busy day, and giving Jesus a little room for His miracle work!

Learning to thank Him during times of difficulty.

Gradually learning to live in a permanent state of trust.

Putting ourselves completely at Jesus's disposal, so that we virtually become miracle-partners with Him.

These, of course, are only a few parts of that growing friendship with Jesus, which naturally lead to His opportunity-taking.

We can notice, perhaps, that the things just mentioned are all to do with closeness . . . a sharing with Jesus of a definite environment. This environment always has a miracle-potential for us.

# 19

# Trust-Miracles

I wonder whether your temperament is a cautious one? My natural reaction was always to see issues in shades of grey, and not to commit myself strongly to any view – and it's still a temptation!

At one time trust wasn't in my vocabulary, especially trust in a supernatural being who couldn't demonstrate why I should trust Him. Anyway, God performed a miracle in this cautious young man some years ago and gave him trust. Arising out of that trust I've seen many wonderful things happen – both in my own life, and in the lives of people with whom I've been involved.

There will be many reading this who, in spite of a "cautious" temperament, and in spite of current problems, realize that they have a sort of persistent and instinctive trust concerning Jesus. That's great – it must be seen as Miracle Number One! The miracle of quiet trust, independent of all reasoning and temperament, always makes our lives ready for God to take further opportunities.

It is as if God, seeing in us a desire to know Him better, "puts into" us something which often completely contradicts our circumstances and our personal make-up. We find ourselves making a decision to trust Jesus, whatever may lie ahead of us. We find ourselves able to say, sometimes surprisingly, "Lord, I'm going to trust *You* from now on!"

The way it usually works is that when trust wavers, as it often will, God, who noted our decision, makes very sure that trust always returns. That trust will be in us as something stable, when our moods fluctuate wildly. Trust will include the things we've mentioned, such as a belief in Jesus as in control of everything, and in His victory over the very real influence of supernatural evil. (We shall look, soon, at our sharing in this victory.)

I'm sure you agree with me that Jesus is the ideal focus for our trust, whether that trust is rock-like or variable! Firstly, of course, His time spent on earth has guaranteed that this is no remote God who can't know "how it feels". Secondly, the divinity of Jesus ensures that it doesn't just stop at knowing how it feels. He is uniquely able to renew whole areas of our lives.

We find that trust is not only extremely useful, but also very beautiful. For example, what do you think of this trusting prayer, which seven-year-old Jane was overheard saying?

> Please Jesus, bless Mummy and Daddy, Auntie Sarah and my dog, Tim. And, dear Lord, please look after Yourself – for if anything happens to You, we're sunk!

I'm sure that Jesus our Lord has many miracles lined up for that particular young lady.

### Trust Through Watching

You will remember how we said that our "view" of Jesus covered two aspects: (a) in creation and (b) in relation to our own life.

119

In the same way, there are two aspects to trusting. Firstly, there is our confidence in His general handling of our life as a whole, and our ultimate destiny. Secondly (and this is harder!), there is our confidence in Jesus in the nitty-gritty of each day – the temptations, the difficult relationships, the irrational fears, the tricky choices.

How does trust become a strong and beautiful thing, the sort to attract miracles? Well, trust starts as a gift, but God then gives us the opportunity to develop that gift so that, in fact, our whole life comes to be based on it. One very helpful thing in developing trust is a sort of monitoring process. We teach ourselves to watch Jesus make things which looked like going terribly wrong, turn out right after all.

It is a good idea, if there is time, to make a note of the problems and difficulties arising each day which we have "given" to Jesus to sort out for us. If we record the way in which these problems are resolved, or how they often just disappear, the list can get very long! We are learning to watch Jesus at work.

All this helps us to go beyond the stage of telling God in our prayers that we trust Him, or beyond the stage of a nice warm feeling of trust from time to time. We enter the stage which Jesus longs to see, of our being able to step out in trust, finding successes where there used to be crushing failures.

## Letting Go

They were trying to rescue young Tony, who was involved in a pot-holing cave disaster. Tony was slowing up the process by reaching out one hand to his would-be rescuers, and waving the other hand frantically against the rocks, looking for something to grip. "No, Tony. Give me *both* hands", said the rescuer, holding out both of his. Tony grasped one and then the other. Rescue completed.

It's sad that so many well-intentioned, churchgoing Christians have areas in which they rely a lot more on themselves than on God, giving Him only one hand, or sometimes no hands at all. It is so easy for trust to be a partial thing, with words of confidence not really acted out. The road to miracles is to reduce steadily those areas in which our trust is only partial, so that Jesus can look at us and say, "Well, there's someone who really *does* have confidence in Me." Give Him both hands, and let Him now take those opportunities!

As we said a moment ago, the life of a person who utterly trusts Jesus is a wonderful thing to see. That life still runs into difficulties, still experiences opposition, still experiences great disappointments, but displays a serenity and an optimism which the world envies. I do hope that we can start, now, watching for those miraculous "coincidences" and noticing the help which so often comes at just the right time.

My hope for each one of us is that the activity of Jesus will now be seen very clearly in our lives – because of our growing trust.

The cynics – maybe even one or two "religious" people of the activist type – may laugh at complete and child-like trust, but that is precisely the sort of trust found in the great saints, and in all their miraculous encounters.

\*     \*     \*

One thrilling thing, of which we gradually become aware, is the mutual nature of a trust relationship with Jesus. We start to realize that He's trusting *us*, that He's not in the least surprised when, in spite of our weakness, we chalk up victories!

A very obvious ingredient of our growing trust is patience, allowing God the space in which to exploit His opportunities. A "trust-situation" between God and ourselves usually involves both patience and a sense of His greatness. Our trust will often mean God letting certain events show us that we've been going ahead of Him a little. On the other hand, a life based on patience does not mean that God always keeps us waiting for a miracle! Since I really trusted Jesus, I've learned to recognize the power-flow into a situation, whenever trust is given.

St Paul, of course, knew all about trust, developed, in his case, in places of danger and hostility. He said:

> We experienced nearly coming to the end of our tether . . . so that we might learn to trust not in ourselves, but in God!

> We know that all the things which happen to us are working for our good, if we love God. These things are all fitting into His plans.

Trust is really a wise gamble on Jesus. There's that lovely illustration of the man who sold all that he had to get a magnificent pearl. He gambled everything on that pearl, and that's what Jesus wants us to do concerning Himself.

Gambling on Jesus – and leaving the way wide open for miracles.

Dear Lord,

Complete trust isn't easy. I look at myself and become discouraged, so often.

But I'm going to start looking instead at You . . . my trust is going to be in what *You* are.

When I'm faced with the challenge of trusting You completely – or not at all – I'm going to choose the former!

My growing trust helps me to thank You now – in advance – for the opportunities You are going to take in my life.

# 20

# Letting-Go Miracles

If you listen carefully to some "pop" records (that's assuming you are clever enough to unscramble the lyrics!), you'll occasionally pick up the phrase "Peace of Mind". Yes, even our teenagers, with lots of exciting things beckoning to them, are searching for that elusive quality.

It's always thrilling to see peace miraculously replacing fear and conflict, and there are two contrasting ways in which it happens.

Firstly, there's the uncanny peace which flows in when something is "lifted" (a burden of guilt, for example) – I've seen this many times.

Secondly, there's the peace which comes when a situation is *not* lifted (has still to be "lived with"), but is now shared by God. This too, I've seen frequently.

Let's look at the first of these areas. Those who are deeply involved in prayer for healing will quickly tell you what is the greatest single barrier against a miracle happening in someone's life. The barrier is that someone is clinging to a resentment; there's an unwillingness, or an inability, to forgive. (Some Christians included, I'm afraid!)

\*     \*     \*

The subject of resentments and forgiveness will, I know, seem a very obvious one! It's worth looking at the subject for a few moments though, because it's not always realized how *many* personalities are miraculously changed in this area of forgiving-and-being-forgiven. It's one of the areas in which God works so beautifully, and produces such amazing and rapid contrasts.

We all know how deep resentments can go. Sometimes, even when we say we have "forgiven" a person who has hurt us, there can still be just a moment's satisfaction in hearing of a misfortune happening to that person! The resentment still lingers, and God will often "light up" this fact for us.

I was talking to a usually affable clergyman, who began to mention one or two people who had opposed what he had tried to do in his last church. Our clerical friend's expression hardened as he said: "Ah, well . . . each one of them is dead now!"

With most longstanding resentments there has been a decision, perhaps almost unconscious, not to forgive a hurt. This decision has changed the whole complexion of life from that point, and drastically affected God's opportunity-scope. The resentment, sadly, has been "hugged" to oneself.

The opposite of "hug", of course, is letting-go, and I have seen some wonderful letting-go miracles. The letting-go, which occasionally needs God's help, has been the signal for an immediate in-flow of peace. Sometimes there is, as well, a disappearance of physical symptoms. But even without the removal of any bodily symptoms, the sense of God's peace is so marvellous that the physical problems have become not quite so important!

\* \* \*

Joan and her daughter Rachel had become bitter enemies after a series of stormy scenes, in a home which later broke up. Joan was temporarily a patient in hospital, and all that happened when Rachel visited was another blazing row. The hurts were very deep.

One day I took them into the quiet little hospital chapel, where they immediately started accusing each other of many awful things. I tried to get in the odd peace-making comment, but that didn't please either party!

It was then that I realized how useless was my "expertise" and so, instead, I said a silent prayer, simply asking Jesus to come and deal with Joan and Rachel.

I can't remember the exact words spoken, but within a few moments mother and daughter were hugging each other, and crying on each other's shoulder. Joan and Rachel were soon on their way out of the chapel, with their arms around each other, and I might as well not have been there! Hugging each other, rather than their grudges.

Jesus, our wonderful Lord, had well and truly, and within seconds, taken an opportunity given to Him.


## Willing?

Sometimes it can seem the most difficult thing in the world to forgive a person who has hurt us badly, even perhaps altering adversely the whole direction of our life. Terribly difficult – almost impossible, unless . . .

Unless, somehow, we can respond to what God is saying to us: "Are you, at least, willing to be made willing?" If, even without any warmth of feeling, we can bring ourselves to say, "Yes, I'm willing", the letting-go process will have begun.

As Jesus increasingly shares our life we shall, of course,

find our love-capacity increasing. It will be His love in us which now helps us to rise above the "natural" bitterness. His presence in us will enable us to stand back a little from the hurt-situation, giving us that Divine perspective for a few moments. We may find ourselves with just a little more understanding about why that person did this to us; or be content in the thought that, at least, God knows and understands.

Soon, if there has been that willingness to let go a resentment, the power of Jesus our Lord can go to the deepest roots of the hurt-area and start to dissolve it. We might even decide, if it's possible, to make a move to heal a relationship, but in any event, the letting-go of our grudge will be a marvellous moment for us. And a marvellous moment for Jesus, too, of course! In our hearts instead of bitterness, there will be peace. It's a peace which so often seems to convey itself to the very next person we meet!

As we let go our grudges, we frequently find that we're letting go some of our scepticism, too. It's as if God melts us not only into relinquishing bitterness, but into a new and warm belief in His care for us. We've come into harmony with the way God intended human existence to be. We *feel* His love for us, more than we ever did, as the grudges disappear.

Letting go resentments, of course, also helps us to get rid of another barrier. Having said "Goodbye" to a grudge, we can, perhaps for the first time ever, feel deeply that God has just swept away things about which we've asked His forgiveness – including, of course, that "unforgiving" attitude of ours!

One of the wonderful things about God's forgiveness of us is the rapidity with which we feel able to make a new start. We were deeply sorry for having hurt Him, above all, and somehow it's as if we're made new again in His eyes. It's as if He now takes the very things by which we hurt Him, and turns them into something positive, making them a place where new and successful effort can begin. In fact, making the forgiveness process a miracle-opportunity.

If we've been really wholehearted, of course, marvellous changes can begin at God's moment of forgiveness, leading to the elimination from our make-up of those tendencies which had hurt Him. And the forgiveness-moment seems to be the signal for the influence of Jesus's love to start bombarding us more strongly than ever.

Under that influence, of course, there is the return of hope, and the sort of peace which needs the adjective "dynamic".

## Guilt Removal

It would be wrong to pretend that the process of forgiving ourselves, after God has forgiven us, is always an easy one.

This is an area in which supernatural evil can have a marvellous time, making us doubt that we've been forgiven, and trying to maintain in us a nagging sense of guilt. (I am increasingly convinced that *this* is the explanation of guilt-after-forgiveness rather than a "morbid" conscience!) God never wants us to carry this burden.

The only way through this problem is a simple decision. We decide that we will ignore all the nagging and all the conflict, and bank upon God's love, accepting that if we were truly sorry, forgiveness is a fact.

Now, I do realize that sometimes guilt can be very deep-seated. Such guilt seems to defy efforts by, say, a priest or minister to "reassure" someone that God has forgiven them. It is, of course, frequently called neurotic guilt.

But God can work a miracle here too! We ourselves can start the process by a systematic "thank You" every time we ask forgiveness for something. About that wrong thing, we can firmly say, "Thank You, Lord, that there's nothing for which to condemn myself, or to punish myself."

I have found that God can make such a lot of this new skill we're learning of emphatically thanking Him that we're forgiven (even if at first it didn't sound too convincing to *ourselves*).

Because there is obviously some limit to what our own "positive statements" can achieve, I believe that God Himself now begins work in those self-condemned areas. Having dealt with the *real* guilt, He's able to say, "That's enough", to those forces whose aim it is to ruin our lives with neurotic guilt.

Proof of God's working is seen when the memory of something wrong we've said or done sneaks back. We now find that the pain which used to accompany such memories has been taken away . . . miraculously!

God's work in those self-condemned areas ensures that each time we now say "Thank You, Lord; there's nothing for which to blame myself", it sounds increasingly convincing to us.

\*　　\*　　\*

Perhaps one fairly obvious thing is worth a reminder because of its great importance. There should always be an immediacy about the two-way forgiveness process. We should never put off, of course, that coming to God with something of which we feel ashamed. Similarly, resentful thoughts of others must be ruthlessly rejected as soon as we find ourselves indulging in them. Both sets of barriers to peace, and to miracles, must stay down!

Although the forgiveness process may appear to be a little compartmentalized (forgiving others – receiving forgiveness – forgiving ourselves), it does, of course, frequently happen that these are virtually simultaneous. The overwhelming sense of God's love carries us through all three in a sort of miracle moment. This occasion has such an impact on us and, for example, on someone who may have been praying with us. It can happen, too, when we're praying on our own!

No human agency, however skilled, however "reassuring", can bring us the wonderful peace of forgiveness; no human agency can give us the ability genuinely to forgive others. Only Jesus, with His love-influence, can do that.

Later, we'll see how peace is given in sad circumstances which look as if they may become even worse.

Dear Lord,

Whenever there's an opportunity to tell someone how much their peace of mind depends on forgiving, and being forgiven, help me to take it.

May I convince someone who is clinging to a deep sense of hurt or bitterness how those barriers against happiness, and against the miraculous, can be removed.

And, of course, Lord, may I never waste time in coming to You for forgiveness myself!

Make me aware of times when resentment is burning in me.

If there is any bitterness there now, I let *You* help me to surrender it, let You lift it away permanently.

Thank You, Lord, that no resentments will hold up Your miracle work in me.

# 21

# Love-Awareness

Here's Bill, aged eighty-nine, but extremely mentally alert.

Bill has that haunted expression of someone who has carried round with him, for many years, a tremendous burden of guilt. There have been things earlier in his life of which Bill feels bitterly ashamed, and although he had a successful career, and has seen his children equally successful, he feels imprisoned by self-blame.

As we talk together about God's love being limitless, I can see that Bill is drinking in every word, just as if it had never really hit him before. I am aware that God is "doing something" in Bill, and the moving little prayer which Bill eventually says has become almost a formality!

Bill doesn't start leaping around the room in ecstasy, but his eager expression shows that God's love now means so much more to him, and that he wants to make the most of the new situation. With the burden lifted, it's as if Bill has been given permission to live.

Bill's awareness of God's love, and the lifting of the pressure of guilt, transform the days which follow, as Bill hungrily reads his Bible, and spends much time in God's company.

Just before his ninetieth birthday Bill becomes ill, and faces a major operation, with all its risk at that age. But Bill writes a marvellous letter, just before the operation, about what a difference living in God's "approval", rather than disapproval, has now made. Bill ends his letter with these words: "I would like to tell you that life, for me, is now wonderful!"

I'm sure that we would all like to feel that towards the end of our life, and facing surgery, we could write like that! God has been lifting Bill above his circumstances, and showing that it's never too late, even at nearly ninety, to take one of those opportunities.

Bill is a marvellous example of what we mentioned earlier: Jesus's presence reversing the frequent process of life worsening as one gets older.

\*     \*     \*

How often you meet people who live in a loveless world. Sometimes, family and friends will have nothing to do with them, and they will end up in hospital after breakdown and, occasionally, a suicide attempt. In some cases, they are people who find it terribly difficult either to give or to receive love.

The sense of isolation is frightening, but it is in such a loveless world that God so often finds His opportunities. The isolation has had to get as bad as it could be and then, perhaps in a strange hospital, God responds to the desperation-sense of one of His children.

One so often sees people taking those early, hesitant steps out of a deep depressive illness when it dawns, for the first time ever, that Jesus loves them. It's as if our Lord drops into those hurt and barren places a consciousness of His care for the person – far more effectively than a chaplain's well-chosen or reassuring words!

This love-awareness more than makes up for all the

coldness, and the experience of being misunderstood. Love begins a quiet miracle-process.

We find that there's a "closeness" and an understanding about Jesus's love which is not there, even in our strongest human relationships. That love helps us to turn away from all the guilt and all the sadness clinging to the years which we feel have been wasted.

We become rather like the criminal who hung alongside our Lord on the Cross – just throwing ourselves upon Jesus's love. Miracle-work in us begins here because, of course, this is no ordinary love. It's the sort of love which says to a person who has failed Him and hurt Him many times: "Yes, my child, I know . . . but I still think the world of you!"

## A New Centre

In most of our lives there's a time when we realize that all our "supports" have disappeared; it can happen very unexpectedly! But into such a situation, into the emptiness, God can bring this miracle-producing awareness of His love, and of His deep concern.

Very frequently, all that we'll have in the world, on the credit side, is a sense of God's love. God's ultimate aim, in fact, is to lift us above circumstances in such a way that we can, at a given moment, find all we need simply in our consciousness of His love. This love-awareness, though it does various things for us, is always peace-producing . . .

The marvellous thing is that the love-awareness need not disappear when a crisis disappears, or when some human support returns. Because an opportunity was given to God in our loveless world, it's as if there is now a permanent bright place at the centre of our life, a place in which we can relax. Everything can now flow from that central place. We start to become lost in that love, and the sharpness of our painful situations is wonderfully reduced.

Living in the consciousness of Jesus's love actually *is* the "new life" about which we have heard so much.

When we arrive at an awareness of Jesus's love in this way and are seen to be relaxing in it, in the midst of things which used to shatter us, friends will probably use the adjective "miraculous" about what has happened to us.

When it registers that we are loved by Jesus, many of us take a long time to get over it! We may have thought that we lacked the "right" temperament, but, all at once, we can't stop ourselves from quietly repeating what is life's most miracle-producing statement: "Jesus loves me!" A statement well worth repeating quietly to ourselves, as Jesus Himself helps it gradually to transform those deep "unconvinced" areas.

That larger-than-life theologian, Karl Barth, went on a world tour of lecturing, and discussing concepts of God with many students. On returning, he was asked about the impressions made upon him. After such a varied experience, in so many countries, what was his overriding thought?

Karl Barth gave a little smile, and said

Jesus loves me, this I know,
For the Bible tells me so.

\* \* \*

Many are bound to be asking, "Can *I* find a stronger awareness of Jesus's love when there are so many discouraging aspects of my present existence?"

I have found that one of the most helpful things is never

to give up just being in His presence, with our varying needs. We may come, initially, with no warmth of feeling, but as we share present needs with Jesus our Lord, the one thing about that "presence", which is never very long in coming through, is love.

It's like spending a lot of time in someone's company, and gradually finding all kinds of nice things about that person.

We start to feel that the "problems" we still have don't matter as much as Jesus's love for us. That love is our guarantee of His work on our behalf, and we sense His love more and more as we start to glimpse instances of that work. The miracle-changes we long for are always brought much closer by letting the thought of His love be in our mind, or never far from it.

That love is always there to come back to when life is hard or when we feel that we've failed. Yes, Jesus our Lord is hurt whenever we fail to take full advantage of that unlimited aspect of His love, and just "let ourselves go" in it.

\* \* \*

The awareness of Jesus's love is a crucial factor in so many aspects of living. Some fairly obvious examples are:

The gradual elimination of fear.

Patience!

A new view of people around us, and how we react to them.

A genuine joy . . . contrasting with a superficial or calculated "brightness".

An end to "self-punishing" ways.

The ability to check a wrong impulse before it's translated into action.

A growing love *for* Jesus, and a growing desire to please Him.

A sense of His love shielding in hostile or demanding
    environments.
An anxiety-free approach to the challenges of each day
    . . . and, of course, miraculous answers to prayers!

I wasn't quite right, was I, in referring to "many aspects of
living"? A realization of Jesus's love for us does, of course,
affect every part of our life! That realization turns out to be
the one priceless thing life can offer, and, of course, one
which will last.

I know we'll find many opportunities each day just to
thank Jesus for the fact of His love.


## Those Deep Wounds

One of the exciting developments of recent years has been
helping troubled people to find healing of their memories.
Love-awareness is the key factor. Those with deep-seated
insecurities (perhaps afraid of close relationships, or
showing all sorts of fear reactions) are prayed for, that the
love of Jesus would touch any painful memories.

Sometimes those painful memories are within consciousness; sometimes, of course, they're quite deeply
repressed. In either case, these are past hurts affecting
present behaviour patterns.

Underlying this ministry of prayer is the fact that God
was, well and truly, aware of our existence, even in the
pre-natal stage ("Before I formed you in the womb, I knew
you"). *All* our painful experiences, therefore, are known
to God. It's when we realize (perhaps years later) that only
*His* help will do, that our situation becomes His
opportunity.

\*    \*    \*

Where there are repressed painful memories, there can be enormous help from having someone who is specialized in this area, praying with us.

But what if we feel that there are these hurt-areas, yet we are not fortunate enough to find the "right" person to pray with us?

I believe that God is not defeated by such a situation. The repression mechanism itself, of course, is part of God's creative process, and would have blotted out intolerably painful things from our consciousness. In a real sense, this was God protecting us. However, I'm certain that when we start to experience God's love, those hurts which adversely affect our life now, and which do *not* serve God's purposes, begin to be removed.

Even a partial realization of the love of Jesus, in someone who seemed to have huge barriers against such an understanding, shows that our Lord is not permanently obstructed by these barriers.

In other words, that very first rather wistful awareness of God's love began a process. As part of that process, I believe that even those locked-away memories, never brought back to consciousness, never specifically "prayed about", are quietly healed as Jesus fills more and more of our life. And I believe that any "exploitation" of those hurt-areas by evil forces is correspondingly restricted.

\*   \*   \*

Often, we ourselves can "invite" Jesus our Lord into those memory areas, whether the hurts are conscious or, perhaps, beyond our recovery.

It's wise to allow plenty of time to relax in His presence, as we do this. What we're doing, of course, is letting our present faith, and sense of His love, come into those frightening or desolate places from the past – with God's help.

Sometimes we can imaginatively re-live our re-membered experiences (times when we were made to feel afraid, or worthless, for example), this time picturing the warm glow of Jesus's love around us as we do so. Standing above the time-process, Jesus our Lord can replace the hurt with a sense of being cared for, and valued, in a way which, even now, we may not fully understand. But the results of inviting Jesus into memories which are either conscious, or assumed to be there, can be amazing.

The invitation to Jesus is something we can repeat, from time to time, of course, because any time spent realizing His love is a valuable one!

In the case of those traumatic experiences completely beyond consciousness, the important thing is that Jesus heals wounds – the barriers are not there for Him.

I am certain that in my own life there were very painful locked-away memories, which used to produce all sorts of fears. These memories were never brought to the surface, but I know that since I've come to know Jesus, there's a much greater sense of security and trust, showing that He has been carrying out a healing process.

None of us are out-and-out experts in this field, but in thinking and praying about this I feel that an awareness of God's love is not necessarily one which erases every painful memory. Some will remain, which God sees as part of our sensitivity, or our maintaining a sense of dependence on Him.

I feel sure, also, that there are some hurt-areas which God does not "automatically" remove without our knowledge. I believe that in these particular areas He "waits" until we have come to know Him a little, so that we shall be certain that our new-found freedom is really from Him. I'm certain that if we just go on focusing on that wonderful love of Jesus, we can leave the matter of our hurt-memories to His great wisdom. He will, I know, heal memory's wounds, according to His unique knowledge of our future needs.

\*   \*   \*

Love is the dynamic of God's opportunity-taking, and it is love which links the various ways in which the world's dark places seem to be illuminated –

Miracles occurring where there is love for *God*.
Miracles where there is love for other people.
Miracles, in the complete absence of the first two, depending solely on His love!

We find that an awareness of Jesus's love is a wonderful link between receiving and giving, if we are His followers. The love which "feeds" us is, of course, the same love which flows out from us. It's worth keeping this indispensable link firmly in mind when we think about being Jesus's miracle-partners.

\*   \*   \*

As a consciousness of God's love grows in us we begin to notice proofs of it every day. Aware that we are loved, we then begin to recognize the things which love is producing – sometimes known only to ourselves!

"Love will find a way" is particularly true when applied to Jesus. Even an imperfect realization of His love is change-bringing and healing. Each moment we spend, consciously, in that love, advances His miracle-work in us.

Lord Jesus,

For a little while, I let go everything but the thought of Your love for me – just as I am. Your love has been hurt many times, and I am sorry for them.

As my thoughts turn to Your love, I let its light shine on all the dark experiences of my life – past and present, remembered or forgotten.

I believe that wounds remembered very dimly, or not at all, are being healed each time I relax in Your love.

I believe something else, as well: that the miracle of *my* loving *You* is taking place, in that awareness of Your love.

Thank You

# 22

# Victory-Miracles

So many remarkable changes occur in people's lives today when they base those lives on the fact that there are supernatural forces of evil, but that God is more powerful than they are!

This way of thinking may take a little getting used to – even for many Christians, who are perhaps accustomed to searching for all sorts of other causes for their problems.

I had to discover the hard way that miracles can only be expected to happen in our lives by taking Jesus seriously. Jesus clearly based all that He did on a certain "view" of existence: evil was an active enemy, trying to disrupt God's creation.

We have already looked at some of the drama which accompanied Jesus's challenging of evil forces. By the way, if supernatural forces were not a factor in the many cases brought to Jesus, the gospel writers must have been terribly mistaken, even if they did naïvely "believe in" such forces, to record Jesus actually commanding those forces to leave. You can understand the disciples mistakenly thinking that they heard Jesus confronting evil on *one* occasion . . . but on so many? If these were mere emotional or physical disorders, would Jesus have wasted His breath on something which was not causative?

Because these forces are still at work, aiming to destroy

people's happiness, and to deflect them from their true destiny, perhaps we could look at some practical ways of overcoming those forces today. By contrast with some of the "passive" miracles, these will involve us taking the initiative a little.

Some might feel that it's an over-simplification, but I am increasingly convinced that underlying all life's phenomena are these two influences: the influence of God's Kingdom (resulting in everything true, peaceful, loving, generous, wise), and an opposing supernatural influence (producing aggressive impulses, fear, pride, error, and human unhappiness generally).

Obviously, we must not make supernatural evil an excuse for the wrong things we do, or the mess we seem to be making of our world. But equally, we are very unwise to ignore its existence.

I'm sure that supernatural evil (existence unsuspected) has been a huge factor in the tragic wars and acts of violence into which people have been driven. Hard to "prove", I know, but Jesus's view of existence – like the rest of the things He told us – makes more and more sense.

\*      \*      \*

It's interesting to listen to some of the causes produced for human problems:

"My father had a violent temper, too."

"I've always had an over-developed super-ego."

"I'm Irish, of course!"

Clearly some things like this are causative to a degree, but it's not the whole picture. There are subtle evil pressures upon us. It's not enough to stop at negative thought patterns; it's not enough even to attribute our problems to a sort of absence-of-God vacuum. It was a long time before I accepted that evil forces really were a factor, but when I did, and allowed Jesus to conquer them with me, what a difference it made!

I realize that some people are morbidly interested in evil. We are wise to forget the morbid preoccupation, but not to forget to use Jesus against a very real, havoc-producing influence.

I spoke to a very likeable doctor who specializes in the difficult field of mental illness. With her training, she realizes that there are complex causes of the troubles with which people come to her – environmental, chemical, hereditary and many, many others. But this doctor, who happens to be a Christian, very firmly believes that there are also problems caused by unseen forces. "Not always easy", she says, "to disentangle the evil-produced and the environmentally-produced . . . but I always proceed on the assumption that in any problem there is some activity by evil forces." This doctor would say, of course, that whatever the source of the trouble (supernatural evil, environmental, or perhaps some of each), God has the answer to it.

\*  \*  \*

I wonder if we could make sure, now, of Jesus doing great things for us in certain areas? Could we couple with that "big" view of Jesus an acceptance, once and for all, that there is an unseen battle of influences upon us . . . but that with Jesus we're on the winning side? I hope we can, because I know that it can't help making a difference, and a miraculous one too!

I have seen the power of evil simply "lifted away" from a

person's life – not by a melodramatic or prolonged exorcism, but by a simple inviting-in of Jesus to break that power. Tears turning to smiles!

When the reality of evil is confronted by Jesus, fearful, imprisoned personalities are released. You can see many "released" people walking around, the lines having disappeared from their faces, looking twenty years younger. *Jesus* has prevented evil from harming them any further.

## The Real Enemy

We don't always recognize an evil influence when people are provocative, unhelpful, hostile, or put obstacles in our way. (Yes, and sometimes they are fellow Christians!)

It's helpful to see a little more deeply and put the blame where it really belongs. Instead of making it a personal hurt, we have a detachment which truly is miraculous as we now start to treat many of those "difficult" friends with love and patience!

It's also useful to remember the deceptive role of evil forces. If we are distracted from God for too long these forces can make us react to circumstances in extreme ways, for example, (1) hasty and compulsive action; (2) paralysing inaction. The main ambition of evil forces, of course, is for us to be unaware of their existence . . . and of God's! There are subtle influences which seem to be a particular danger for those who are trying to follow Jesus. They include:

Spiritual pride (it just *has* to be first).
Fearful indecision.
Oppressive guilt.
Blindness to the true nature of a situation.

Unwise, untrusting action.
Confusion.
Discouragement.
Preoccupation with other people's imperfections.

Lots more, of course, and each of us more vulnerable to some than to others! It's also wise to see as temptations some of the things which "darken" our mood, such as doubt, violent dislikes, despondency, apprehension . . . temptations leading, often, to our adversely affecting others' lives.

## *Using Jesus's Victory*

Although there are people who may need intensive prayer for the removal of a particularly strong hold on them by evil, the good news is, of course, that we ourselves can use His victory, a victory which He longs to share with us.

This will sound familiar to many, I know, but countless miracle changes would have resulted from the much wider recognition that evil is completely powerless when Jesus and we are united against it. Yes, it is a war-situation, but the "weapons" which Jesus's followers need for winning are already in their hands. Jesus, in fact, has won for us a very real freedom from evil's subtle holds on us, if only we will use that freedom.

For those who are not consciously doing so, it could revolutionize life to accept the real source of so much of our unhappiness, and to use Jesus's victory-by-freedom against it. In this way we become a small but vital part of the overall cosmic victory which God is winning.

Watch how a consciousness of our freedom can affect the choices of each day. I know that it doesn't sound terribly sophisticated, but our "thank You, Lord, for victory" in some decisive choice will carry us through, where before we used to fail miserably.

Obviously we all make exceptions in resisting evil's pressures (I know I do). Our aim must be to make that resistance total if we can, in order to reduce our vulnerability. This may seem hard to achieve, but the victories which God leaves for us to win are, in fact, always within our capacity. For His part, He's working for us all the time to divert things which literally could destroy us. Because we initially asked God to share our life we can take it for granted that there are victories being won on our behalf, all the time, of which we are completely unaware. Scores of little miracles happen when there's a "Jesus-can-help-me-with-this-one" attitude. It's also vital to think of the victorious aspect of Jesus's love! Because His love is essentially an influence, we'll be amazed how that influence, when we focus on it, proves stronger than the apprehension, the guilt, the doubt, the panic, which evil is trying to implant. We find that He does what we expected Him to do . . . and this all helps our miracle-recognizing ability no end!

Eventually we can even be glad when conscious of being pressurized by evil because we know that it's yet another opportunity to show how free we are!

Jesus told us that we could start being optimistic because of His victory over the world's sources of trouble. What He's saying to each one of us is, "You're right to take the forces opposed to Me very seriously, but don't be afraid of them. If I'm with you, the very worst that evil can throw at you cannot cause harm."

## Immediate Refusal

Just a word about those negative feelings and reactions which we have grown to think are part of us.

The way to eliminate these things (quite miraculously, in many cases) is to see them, instead, as intruders. Recognizing an intrusive challenge by evil in things which were "habitual", we can now immediately refuse to permit their continuance. It's as if we are saying to feelings of panic, despair, guilt, anger, acute anxiety, self-pity, "You can't intrude here", as we use Jesus's victory.

Many find it helpful to feel a sort of rock-like quality, shared with Jesus, about their resistance to evil's pressures. Others are helped by seeing Jesus as a shield against those pressures.

I won't pretend that there's not a little effort involved in all this! The effort of choosing is sometimes made against terrific pressure, but Jesus blesses that effort and always "completes" that victorious moment for us. Using the victory of Jesus changes us; it changes others (sometimes hostile) around us; it changes potentially dangerous situations.

Many people find that evil's pressure can be crowded out by plunging into absorbing things – outdoor and active, or perhaps lovely music or a riveting story! If these things are combined with a trusting, joyful and praising attitude towards Jesus in the fluctuations of each day, evil finds it much more difficult to intrude.

\*　　\*　　\*

A final and fairly obvious reminder: *Evil never gives up!* we can expect a constant attempt to frustrate that closer relationship with God. But although the pressure on us may be constant, so, of course, is the supply of power. Using that power (i.e. involving Jesus) literally transforms evil's activity into miracles of victory.

As we thank Him for victory, we are increasingly able to refuse all negative things, and somehow the world seems a little brighter with each win which Jesus and we pull off!

How many more miracles of victory there would have been if these principles had been followed:

Don't be morbidly preoccupied with evil, or overawed by it, but do *take it seriously*.

Don't be afraid of it.

Remember that evil is scared stiff of the presence of Jesus!

---

Lord Jesus,

May my life be firmly based, always, on the realities of existence which You made so clear. I accept that so much of the conflict which You said would come to Your followers originates in a cosmic influence, aiming to wreck human happiness.

I'm going to make sure that I am united with Your own invincibility. As I do so, I know that evil will be powerless in my life. I know that as I resist those pressures and choose new reactions to them, You are going to complete each victory for me.

Thank You, Lord Jesus, that there is going to be a miracle now: my being a defeated person no longer!

---

# 23

# Darkness Shared

"How can she be so calm?"

As well as the miracle of peace when a tremendous weight such as guilt is lifted, there is another peace-miracle when burdens such as illness and severe handicap are *not* lifted, and circumstances are *not* changed.

How can Mary, here in this wheelchair, having had one set-back after another, be so serene, and talk about how good God has been to her? How can Ian, terminally ill, but very aware of everything, talk so hopefully, in spite of realizing that things couldn't be worse?

\* \* \*

As we said earlier, God uses a suffering world as a unique setting for His miracles – the emergence of hope against all reason; courage replacing a fear which seemed natural and "justified" by the circumstances; people amazing their friends by an optimism and placidity never previously seen.

Although so many outward circumstances of our lives don't change, one finds Jesus our Lord, with great skill, taking the opportunity of our crises, our conflicts, and our limiting factors. There is absolutely no human situation, however dark, which God cannot bring into harmony with His purposes of love – even though the darkness may have to be endured for a time.

You will have read of the miraculous changes which have happened in those who have come through almost unbearable places with Jesus. No matter what their temperament used to be, they acquired a peace which could not be shaken.

Sceptical people may say – "Oh, this is just the old stuff about God using our sufferings and bringing good out of them." Well, they may say it if they wish, but I've seen God using the opportunity of life's handicaps and tragedies in sometimes incredible ways, many many times.

Darkness can descend on us so quickly, can't it? The loss of someone greatly loved, the news (perhaps with no previous warning signals) that we ourselves may not have very long to live . . . In circumstances like these, even longstanding Christians, being only human, can find their faith crumbling.

And even if faith remains, there may be no desire to "share" this with God – as one Christian lady whose dreams had just been shattered said, "I just wasn't talking to God any more!" And so, for a friend to try to "justify" God's purpose at such a time could be worse than saying nothing at all.

## The Crucial Involvement

When tragedy comes, or an ambition, which we were sure God shared with us, suddenly disintegrates, there may be no desire at all to "invite" God into this new and dark situation.

It will seem impossible to see beyond the present crisis

to any place of safety or happiness again. We literally shrink from what the coming days are going to bring. It is precisely at this point that the miracle of peace can begin . . . not when things "improve", not when things are "adjusted to" but *now*.

We have probably got used to "bringing in" Jesus as a first, rather than a last, resort when things go wrong. But now, here's a really terrible and overwhelming situation. Can we still do it? Can we, through our tears, or sense of numbness, still "bring in" Jesus? Can we, even with no real hope that it will make any difference, invite Him in?

Yes, it often is a huge effort. We could, in fact, be turning to the Lord in the midst of temporary anger with Him, angry that He would let this happen. But that turning to Him is an instinctive acknowledgement that He is still the only hope for us. It's as if we are responding to God's gentle request, "My child, I know it's dark there. Can I come in?"

Our risen Lord, incomparably loving and understanding, is *there*, whatever the degree of our realization of it. And soon we may become dimly aware of something which almost contradicts our present situation, a sense that it is being shared.

There is still a continuing, painful realization of what has happened (no magical "taking away" of this), but into it all, ever so gently and gradually, comes just a little of the peace of heaven.

We may never have experienced this peace before – even in the most "favourable" circumstances – but this tumbling-in of our world was Jesus's opportunity. The peace which mingles with the dread and the heartbreak means that the Lord of History happens to be involved right now. He is feeling our pain to an even greater degree than we do ourselves. Peace has come, not through our feeble effort of thought or desire or, perhaps, from someone else's "comforting words", but because of the reality of a Presence.

## Sharing and Healing

Paul said, "If you bring your situation or present needs to God, His peace will be yours. It is a peace which is far above human analysis. That peace will be like a sentry . . . standing guard over your deepest being, as you just rest in Jesus." How typical of Jesus our Lord that so often when suffering is greatest, He bestows His greatest gift, saying: "I know that this seems almost unbearable for you. I am feeling it, too, and deeply sharing it with you. I will bring you through this dark place . . . and all the time you can feel completely safe in My love."

The peace of Jesus our Lord is at work at a deeper level than our present anxious reasoning-processes. A glimpse of that bright future, against all "reason", so often projects itself into where we are now, even if only for a second or two.

We shall, of course, be devastated by the finality of the *cause* of the hurt remaining (a loved one will not be coming back to us . . .), but His peace will be exerting a healing influence on the hurt itself. Also, there will be an awareness that the risen Jesus is ahead of us, preparing to meet the need of each of the following days. We shan't be facing those days on our own.

The change which comes into a situation shared by Jesus accounts for the contrast between the "hopeless" circumstances of a believing person, and the attitude of that person. Observing this contrast, an onlooker will so often think, "This is remarkable" or even, of course, "It's miraculous".

I am terribly conscious that what I am saying about the presence of Jesus in dark places could sound, for some, a little too "smooth". I can only say that I have seen Jesus our Lord transform countless dark situations, which have been opportunities for Him. That Presence has made a difference for which "miraculous" is the only word.

\* \* \*

The gentle speaking of our Lord's Name, which we thought of earlier, is, of course, particularly helpful during times of great crisis. Perhaps the whole world has collapsed around us, but we may *just* manage to whisper "Jesus".

**Jesus** . . . even though part of me would willingly die right now.

**Jesus** . . . this experience is overwhelming, but I'm still clinging to Him.

**Jesus** . . . I shrink from facing what is ahead, but I'm dimly aware of someone holding me.

**Jesus** . . . I can scarcely think, but, as I say His Name, I can believe for a moment that this present darkness will not last.

**Jesus** . . . before the trauma of all this can bury itself in my mind, it is surrounded by His peace.

**Jesus** . . . with a superhuman effort I look away from this dark place, and the thought of Him tells me that there must be a brighter day.

**Jesus** . . . and I am absorbing something of Him with which to get through the coming days.

It's good to remind ourselves, from time to time, that God already stands at those crisis-places in our future. We don't know what form these crises will take, but we know that He will be there. God will use the opportunity to transform those places; He will use them to bring us closer to knowing Him – rather than their being faith-destructive crises.

Using a world just like this, Jesus our Lord miraculously develops in people things like courage, empathy, and knowledge of Himself. These, of course, are things we will keep . . . to carry forward from our present existence.

Dear Lord,

Please help me to live by one vital truth: that what really matters is not "fortune" or "misfortune", but Your sharing.

May that Presence, and that sharing, be a light (even if only a glimmer) when darkness comes over my life.

When I am afraid, or when I am experiencing great loss or sorrow, may I find my security, instinctively, in You.

Help me to remember what You have prepared for those who trust You. Let that unique hope project itself into present heartbreaks, or doubt of You . . . to bring with it the miracle of peace.

Thank You

# 24

# Miracles of Looking

We thought earlier about Peter taking those remarkable steps on Galilee Lake.

One sentence in the report of that incident is vital concerning Jesus taking lots of opportunities in our lives today. Here it is: "When Peter took his eyes off Jesus, he began to sink."

Just as a miracle was actually taking place in that few seconds while Peter looked trustingly towards Jesus, so there's a very real miracle-potential for *us*, whenever we can look away from ourselves and towards Him.

By the way, those other miracle-producing factors (the awareness of God's love, the increase of our trust, the using of Jesus's victory) are all helped by the "looking" process!

\*   \*   \*

Keeping our mental gaze upon Jesus is not an unreal or strained exercise, reserved for the more advanced in monasteries or convents. Our "look" is a natural safeguard against the facts of this life becoming much more real than the fact of God's presence. It helps us to realize what already exists – His closeness to us.

If we say that God guides us, it makes good sense to

keep an eye upon our guide. And, of course, in learning to notice God's activity on our behalf, it makes sense to be giving Him our attention. So much of His quiet miracle-work can be missed if we are, for too long, "looking the other way".

In a very relaxed way, our look can help us to maintain a virtually unbroken sense of the presence of Jesus our Lord. For example, some find it helpful simply to picture His light surrounding all that they do. Others focus on a "presence" of compassion and understanding. In very demanding or frightening circumstances there may be a mental picture of Jesus encircling us with those outstretched arms (this one, for example, is very useful just before going to sleep).

As each day we practise keeping our eyes on Jesus, as far as possible, any initial sense of unreality soon disappears, and the process becomes instinctive. As the focus of our attention moves away a little towards Jesus it usually brings a heightened awareness of two things in particular: (1) His unwavering love for us, and (2) His control (i.e. He is coping!)

The way in which we practise the vital new art of looking in a heavenly direction will vary with individuals, of course, but will usually result in a sense of God's real involvement in each day's details.


## On Course

Keeping our eyes on Jesus obviously doesn't mean being completely unaffected by the inevitable relationship problems, and all that's involved in living in this uncertain world. But that awareness of His presence does seem to bring an immunity from the more devastating and lasting harm produced by those evil forces we thought about.

God would, of course, protect us from so many things anyway, but that "look" makes a tremendous difference. There's usually a quicker response to danger, for example.

Focusing on Jesus is like watching a steady light when everything around us is so confused, and this is one of the reasons why our look gives us a much clearer sense of direction. We make fewer mistakes! We surprise ourselves (and others who have known us for a long time), by the successful choices we now make. Going through life with this supernatural dimension means that we have a greater sense of safety. But it's not just a case of imagining that we're safe. In the things that really matter, we *are* safe.

As we look towards Jesus, He too is receiving. From us, He receives the great satisfaction of our growing love, trust and gratitude.

We find, in practice, that the speaking of Jesus's Name, and the "look" in His direction blend beautifully! We whisper His Name . . . trustingly, affectionately (perhaps in a fear-situation), and instinctively we focus on that light, that aura of love, that understanding smile, or whatever is our own visual reminder of His presence.

Does maintaining a sense of the presence of Jesus diminish the attention or the love which we can give to other people? No, it does not! The people we are with, in fact, benefit, because there is now a new dimension to our contact. We bring to our encounter with someone a real influence.

Miraculous changes in our personalities can occur when we learn to take our eyes off threatening present circumstances and look, instead, in Jesus's direction. We can't completely ignore the circumstances, of course, but in them we begin to show a steadiness and a courage which were not there previously.

Resolutely to look away from the stress-producing aspects of a situation and towards Him is a well-known and longstanding piece of advice to Christians, but one that is, I'm afraid, terribly neglected.

\*   \*   \*

As we focus on Jesus our Lord there grows, each day, a sense of being united with Him. We become certain that Jesus and one of His children who trusts Him, are inseparable. United – you can imagine how this revolutionizes our meeting of various challenges. The glance to Jesus, and the realization of that unity, encourages us to attempt new things. It is now "we", rather than the hesitant "I". I'm sure that Jesus also sees that look from us as anticipatory. We are ready for the next little miracle He is going to accomplish, and provided that we leave the choice to Him, He'll make sure that our expectant look has a result!

In those sudden fierce temptations, or when we're aware that we are "manufacturing" wrong or unloving thoughts, it's now much easier (if we have acquired the looking habit) simply to picture Jesus lifting us above these things. We find miraculous new reactions, perhaps realized only by ourselves, as we "see" Jesus helping us to rise above negative ways.

There is not only the victorious aspect, of course, but the process of illumination, as we keep our gaze upon Jesus. So often, as we do so, He will lovingly show us one or two things which need changing. This is usually by the encouraging sense of His help in bringing about those changes, a "with-Me-you-can-do-it" sense.

Yet another aspect of looking towards Jesus is that of our submission. We're really looking at Him and saying, in effect, "Have it *Your* way, Lord." That look of acceptance, a sort of relinquishment, has brought about many miracles. People have "surrendered" to God something on which they have set their hearts, in case it was not, for the moment, at least, what He wished for them. Frequently, this has resulted in the eventual arrival of the thing longed for – and in a far better way than could have been imagined. It's as if our look of acceptance, of "wanting what God wanted", released God's power to bring about the desired thing – and frequently other blessings as well.

The submissive look can bring from God what strident demands fail to bring, if we genuinely wanted only what is pleasing to Him.

* * *

Just to sum up a few of the results of keeping our eyes on Jesus:

Our look . . . always increasing the sense of His love.

Our look . . . lifting us above the things which used to disturb us.

Our look . . . giving us a basic sense of safety.

Our look . . . encouraging Jesus to work on the day's details!

Our look . . . giving us the sense of His understanding.

Our look . . . saving us from many disastrous choices.

Our look . . . changing the view of present circumstances into a calmer one.

Our look . . . helping us to see, more clearly, His interventions.

Our look . . . increasing the sense of our inseparability from Jesus.

Our look . . . seeing the road ahead, without the usual visual obstructions.

Our look . . . and the "prayer department" of our life seems to be growing into something almost continuous!

There will be many other rewarding aspects of looking in Jesus's direction, which we shall discover for ourselves.

---

Dear Lord,

In many ways it's "natural" to look at the problems! It's "natural" to focus on the worldly dimension, and to forget the supernatural one.

I will try, with Your help, to cultivate the supernatural habit . . . looking to You, until it becomes instinctive.

Thank You for all the changes which will come from keeping my eyes upon Yourself.

# 25

# Thank-You Miracles

It's amazing how we can be aware, as Christians, of an important habit (even agreeing warmly with practising it), and yet neglect to make full use of it. One of the most thrilling ways of ensuring that God can take opportunities in our lives has been known for at least three thousand years.

Long before St Paul wrote about "thanking God in all circumstances", the writers of Psalms showed that this was part of their way of life too.

In the present day, a former U.S. Army chaplain, Colonel Merlin Carothers, has been among those to explore the "thanking for everything" theme. Merlin saw many wonderful things happen to people who, after at first being sceptical, started thanking God, even for their problems. This meant that God's opportunity-potential could be realized.

John Wesley believed that you just could not separate real prayer and thanksgiving. "The person who prays, blesses God for all things . . . looks on them all as coming from Him", he wrote.

The great William Law, in the nineteenth century, said, "Thank and praise God for everything that happens to you. If you thank God for seeming disasters, you turn them into blessings" . . . or opportunities!

Underlying the wise advice we've just read, of course, is the recognition that God is in control. He won't let anything come into the life of someone who trusts Him if it cannot, in some way, serve a good purpose. This includes even the heartbreak situations. We are not, of course, thanking God for bad things for their own sake, nor voicing our approval of them. What we are doing is thanking Him for what He is bringing, or will bring, from the misfortunes. And what He brings is, so often, a miracle!

Now, is it easy?

Well, like many others, I found the thanksgiving habit very hard at first. "Am I supposed to thank God for *this*? What possible purpose can He have in allowing *this*?" So I did say "thank you", but very mechanically.

Gradually it dawned on me that Paul was absolutely right when he advised, "Whatever happens, be thankful for it." Mind you, I'm sure that Paul's advice was not offered as a sort of magic formula for miracles, even though it so often seems to work that way! Paul just had an overwhelming sense of gratitude for having been "rescued" by God. He could take in his stride the hard things, because he had life's one priceless gift . . . Jesus.

Cynical people may say that thanking God for every circumstance is just a bit of sound psychology, which merely changes your outlook, and makes events seem as if an unseen hand is at work. Don't believe that "explanation", because it's completely inadequate! When you make it a habit – even when shattered by some event – to say "Thanks, Lord, for allowing this to happen", things far beyond coincidence can occur. The trusting expression of thanks brings into play spiritual forces which, transcending natural cause-and-effect, turn reverses into advantages.

After we've thanked God for some misfortune, a positive factor in the situation will so often light up for us. A friend may ring at just the right moment, or we'll be aware that the courage we needed to deal with this has suddenly come. There will usually be some personality gain, as God uses these circumstances.

It's as if God is saying to Himself – "This child of Mine has thanked Me for this – and so I'll make sure that the thanks are justified."

## There's a Purpose

As we thank God as a discipline (and we may need His help in doing this sometimes), we so often see Him entering the situation in remarkable ways. This intervention may be quite soon, or it may be gradual. If it is gradual, almost imperceptible at first, then there'll be a purpose in the timing, and it's wise just to go on thanking.

So many of the things which we experience, of course, are not in the sphere of illness or sad personal loss. We may be trying to adjust to a "difficult" marriage partner, an exacting boss, a teenage son or daughter who seems determined to break our heart . . .

The advice is still the same: Thank God that He has some good purpose in allowing this. As Paul once said in effect: "I don't understand all that God is sending my way . . . including the pain . . . but I thank Him for it." It's rather like the learner saying about the expert, or the child about the father, "Well, I'm sure he knows best."

I do realize, of course, that it must sound almost like lying to ourselves to thank God for things which at times are devastating. The "thank you" simply won't come. We would much rather be thanking Him for changing these circumstances than using them.

Perhaps we can get a little closer to thanking, even with breaking heart, along the line of trust. In our shattered state, there may be a moment when we're *just* able to say, "Lord, this is terrible. You have allowed it – I can't think why . . . yet I know that You love me."

At such a moment, God can help us through the tremendous effort of thanking Him for what He will do with this situation, thanking Him with trembling voice, and with all light having gone from our life.

I remember when something happened which I felt I could never "get over" I managed (just) to thank Jesus, that because He had allowed it, it would serve some good purpose. It was quite soon that I noticed a growth in courage, as well as a sense of not being as dependent as I used to be on circumstances. I believe that the Lord has vital personality gains ready for us in every dark situation.

If we are doing our best to live close to Jesus, and painful situations occur, we can be absolutely certain that He would not have allowed them if they could not, in some way, push forward the perfect design He has for us.

If a situation continues unchanged, it won't always be easy to keep on thanking God for it. But it's important to maintain the thanks, believing with all our heart that He is responding to the opportunity which our first "thank you" gave to Him.

It will be a little easier to thank God for difficult circumstances if we are already thanking Him for the many instances of His care for us during each day. That almost automatic thank-you response can extend to cover every aspect of our life, and brings about some marvellous changes in us. We find that we are acquiring the skill of recognizing an opportunity of some kind in a disadvantage, or in a limiting factor. Helen Keller, who was terribly handicapped but achieved so much, used to say, "I thank God for my handicaps . . . through them I have found myself, my work, and God's love."

The thanking-God-for-everything habit is, of course, very much tied up with the theme of our book: becoming expectant, and miracle-aware. Our new awareness of His activity in the every-day details means that the words "Thank you" are often being whispered to Him. I must admit that I find myself saying lots of little "thank you's" throughout each day, in a sort of cycle of recognition and gratitude. I wish I'd done it earlier!

\* \* \*

When we're quite unable to feel any affection for someone who has hurt us badly, let alone to thank God for "allowing" the hurt, we can frankly tell Him so. Once again Jesus our Lord can help us to say that "thank you" . . . accompanied, so often, by a disappearance of the grudge!

It's important to notice that when we say, "God has allowed this, so He must have some good purpose in it", it is never a pathetic resignation. That thankful attitude means a release of God's miracle-power, and soon positive things will be seen to be happening.

It's interesting to see what so often happens when a frustrating or unexpected thing which looks like spoiling the day becomes, instead, the subject of thanks. The "thank you" moment seems to be a signal for all sorts of helpful and "convenient" things to follow – if we're looking out for them.

## *Planned!*

God is never restricted to merely "salvaging" a difficult situation. There is, so often, the aspect of His initiative. It reminds us of Joseph in the Old Testament. His brothers engineered his being carted off to Egypt as a slave, but later when they met him, they were full of remorse. Joseph magnanimously told them: "You can forgive yourselves! You plotted something bad – but God meant it for good – a long time back" – as subsequent events proved.

Unless God sees it as serving some useful purpose, He simply won't tolerate our being unfairly treated, or slandered, or obstructed. So if we find that we've been the subject of a little character assassination, we can thank Him!

One of the great joys of learning the thanksgiving habit is when we discover that we're meeting, in an entirely new way, situations which used to shatter us completely. As one lady said, "When things go wrong, I just say a 'thank you' to Jesus now. Nothing has the power to upset me as it used to do."

Thanking God for the difficult places is just part of the generally miracle-producing effect of gratitude, of course. Those people in whom we can see the miracle of "joy-despite-circumstances" are usually grateful people above everything else, aren't they?

The gratitude-response always seems to be anticipating some good thing, bad as the situation is at the moment. There is a miracle-expectancy which is never completely lost, even when things are at their very worst.

The gratitude-response is based on the *fact* of God, and the absolute conviction that He can't fail us. And, in a still largely indifferent world, we can just imagine what our "thank you" does for Him!

Our gratitude is more than an automatic response, of course, it is praising God for His own sake, quite irrespective of what He may be allowing.

Thank you, Paul, and others, for that miracle-working advice!

Dear Lord,

I express to You my complete trust in Your control of the circumstances of my life.

There have been many dark places which I see, now, as serving Your purposes. There have been other things for which I still can't see the reason . . . but I thank You for them.

Thank You for every painful, or unwelcome, or problem area of my life right now. I surrender myself to Your perfect use of those areas.

I do thank You that You are very much at work in all the difficult circumstances which I may have given to You. In some, I can detect Your use of those things; in others I still can't!

I am grateful that in a world like this I have life's one unchanging and priceless gift . . . You Yourself.

Thank You that, even now, You are causing the circumstances of my life to bring about the miracle-changes You have planned for me.

# 26

# Our Guest

In case "intervening" sounded a bit like God jumping into a situation from outside, perhaps it's worth reminding ourselves of His constant interior work! Jesus did, of course, promise us that He would live *in* His followers.

Religion is often made a little more complex than it needs to be. I hope that I'm not adding to the complexity by saying that if our lives are centred on Jesus, then God's Holy Spirit most certainly lives in us, working out a sort of miracle-blueprint for us.

The tough and often slow job of making us what He wants us to be is carried out by the risen Jesus, living in us now by His Holy Spirit. Don't ask me to disentangle them!

I'm sure that Jesus and the Holy Spirit are so inseparable that if someone says, ecstatically, "The Holy Spirit fills my heart", Jesus our Lord isn't offended; and that when someone says, "What a difference Jesus has made", the Holy Spirit won't be hurt!

\*    \*    \*

We don't always realize what a tremendous miracle-opportunity was given to God at the very first moment that we turned, hesitatingly, in His direction. It's not just a platitude, to encourage someone who's waiting patiently for a miracle, to say that God *took* that opportunity. It means everything to Him when someone recognizes how much they need Him, and promises to try to trust Him.

The vital thing is that as soon as that turning to Him is made – and we each do it in distinctive ways – He is able to see that hesitant or mixed-up child of His as already perfect.

"Oh no, not another of those flights of fancy!" Well, it may seem a little unrealistic, until we remember:

(1) God's love, and
(2) His knowledge of the future.

In His love, our Lord builds everything upon that first opportunity. It may seem a little rash of Him, but that's the way He is. God sees our perfection beyond all the spiritual struggles, the shattering failures which lie ahead of us.

The reason for the miracle-changes, of course, is identification. The reason why Jesus chose to live in us by His Spirit as well as to exist around us is because of His wish to go on sharing human experience in the closest possible way. It is a continuation of His experience when on earth but now, of course, much wider.

Because the life of Jesus now interpenetrates ours (without cancelling out our personalities), so much of what we express is also expressive of Him. As His work advances in us, the people who are drawn to us are really being drawn to Him; our reactions become, increasingly, His.

There's a growing wisdom because of this identification. We shall understand people, seeing what lies behind their actions, and make fewer mistakes in our handling of them.

Identification also means, of course, that the indwelling Jesus experiences uniquely all our sorrows, longings and disappointments.

The work of God's Spirit in us is one which we feel more able to take for granted than His work in response to requests for His "intervention". His opportunity-taking seems more natural, because He's already resident!

Sadly, we can exist as Christians for many years without really drawing upon resources which the Spirit of Jesus within us would have made available. Drawing upon the strength already there, would have avoided repeated failures.

## Expanding

The more we welcome the work of God's Spirit in us, the faster will be the progress towards that new person God sees.

Paul said that when the Spirit of Jesus lives in us we're able to have a freshness in all that we do or think. Things like optimism, patience, courage will be found, where until then we used to look for them in ourselves without success. New ways of living, for the choosing.

Perhaps at first we'll just accept a little mechanically, that Jesus is carrying out His interior work in us, that He's starting to take opportunities. But if we are patient, we'll soon be able to feel the results of His work. We'll be conscious of Jesus expanding in us – causing us to think and react in ways which surprise us.

We will see changes which we know could only have been brought about by Him.

We'll recognize that the person who now confronts those longstanding problem areas (and problem people!) is rather different. Because of His love, He ensures that we never completely lose that desire for more of Himself, and it's this desire which ensures His constant work in us. He will use all sorts of life experiences to advance that work.

"Perfect? If He can do that for me it will certainly be a miracle to end all miracles . . ."

Yes, but God accepts the challenge!

We have become His responsibility, and can be certain that as long as we're not deliberately turning our back on God, His Spirit is carrying out vital interior work. This work will show itself as those lasting miracle-changes of personality.


## New Person

The work of the Holy Spirit in us is really that of making harmony and making new.

"When someone becomes a Christian," said Paul, "he becomes a brand-new person inside." On the surface there may not seem to be much change at first, but deep in us – where it matters – a momentous change has been made. And God is the first to see it!

**God's Spirit** starts healing some of those deep mental and spiritual "wounds".

**God's Spirit** starts to give us a sense of never being alone.

**God's Spirit** ensures that we actually share Jesus's nature, and start growing more like Him.

**God's Spirit** starts making something of those latent talents.

**God's Spirit** loosens the grip of things which aren't for our ultimate benefit.

**God's Spirit** steadily advances the plans which Jesus has for us.

**God's Spirit** starts to produce those quiet miracles (but not too quiet for our friends eventually to start noticing!)

It seems to help along God's miracle-work if we can regularly thank Him for some of the things just mentioned . . .

Thank You, Lord, that You're healing my wounds.
Thank You, Lord, that You're developing my talents.
Thank You, Lord, that You're setting me free from things which obstruct our relationship.

\* \* \*

We can now, in fact, *be* that changed person because the forces which would oppose this, and push us back into the old ways, are already defeated. The Person responsible for that victory is now part of us! And, above everything else, the work of Jesus within makes us much more aware than we would otherwise be of how much He *loves* us.

\* \* \*

Recorded at the very end of the Bible is Jesus saying, "I am making everything new." That sums it up.

Jesus's presence in us can only be a miracle-working presence. Instead of looking anxiously to see whether we're changing, we can simply thank Him that the making-new process is taking place!

Lord,

Thank You that long before I really trusted You, You put Your confidence in me.

Thank You that You saw what I could become.

As You live in me, I realize that there's nothing which You can't put right.

I'm glad to accept all that You are doing. Don't let me slow it down.

I'll use the strength which is now part of me and just turn my back on those old ways of failure.

Because You live in me, I know that the things which I see in You (love, serenity, courage, patience) must be growing in me . . .

Thank You

# 27

# Those Miracle-"Dates"

It's a very obvious thing (though not always acted upon), that God's miracle-activity is terribly restricted if we don't make enough time for Him, if we haven't acquired the habit of arranging little "dates" with Him at all sorts of odd times. Opportunity-times!

Sad that all the resources of heaven are, as they say, just a whispered prayer away, and yet we find so many "busy" Christians not pausing sufficiently really to draw upon those resources. It's not surprising that His closeness is not felt, when we leave Him out of so many aspects of life.

It is a unique time for God to take the opportunities in our current situation when we set aside even the briefest period just for Him. Our ingenuity in watching for chances for a "date" with Jesus (perhaps hastily arranged) can be wonderfully rewarding.

Lives have been given a completely new direction when Jesus has been allowed to use some time snatched from a hectic day. I believe that Jesus is constantly prompting us to make time for Him. When *we* start getting the same objective there are going to be many of those little miracle-dates!

Experienced Christians often forget that time deliberately spent with Jesus our Lord (yes, even putting aside our pursuit of some urgent "religious objectives" for a few minutes) is the most vital thing we can be doing. As soon as we're getting so busy with His cause that we seem to be losing *Him*, it is time for one of those short and secret meetings! If we are telling the world that there is a spiritual dimension, then it's worth spending a little more time in enjoying it.

The important thing about creating times like this is that the barriers to His influence are temporarily lifted, we're opening the doors and allowing peace to return, allowing insights to be given.

Making a quiet opportunity-time for God is not opting out of life, of course, but just getting a little closer to what life is all about. Like the date with someone of whom we are very fond, these times in the presence of Jesus increasingly become occasions to which we eagerly look forward.

### *Excuse, Please . . .*

The conversation over our fifteen-minute coffee-break this morning seems to be increasing our tensions, it's giving us one or two new things to worry about! This could be the moment, very politely, to excuse ourselves. Still clutching our coffee mug, we intend to have a minute or two "receiving" from Jesus instead.

This switching-off of the world, with its disturbing impressions, is not just escapism, and it's not just the creation of a vacuum. Positive things start to happen the moment we are consciously with Him. Even a minute or two is a renewal process, infinitely greater than that obtained from just physically resting. And there is *no* location where a little communion with God proves impossible.

We don't always realize the depth of what is received when we create even a short time to be with Jesus. We are, of course, relaxing in what He is. So often there is the return of a wonderful sense of security and steadiness, as the Fatherhood of God reaches us, through Jesus our Lord, at such times.

There is a process not only of renewal, but of inspiration. He'll be popping into our heads one or two wise directions for the coming hours, as we fade out our own often confused intellects.

This brief time might be used to share with Jesus one or two things which have gone wrong so far today (they usually do!), or we may be happy just to enjoy the sense of His love surrounding us. We can use the time, of course, to bring to Him the needs of people we know. As our thoughts turn in a Jesus-direction, we begin to get some of our priorities right. Solutions to some very stubborn problems can light up as we caress that mug of coffee, in His presence. We may begin to see the way forward for a loved one, or a friend.

In a largely unconscious process, this time with Jesus means more and more of Him in our own nature. No wonder that so many of the world's decisive miracles have started quietly, during a snatched "date" with Jesus – a burst of courage, a flash of insight, which was not there three minutes earlier, a quiet mood-change, which later led to someone making a tremendous impact on the society of their day. Miracles may not have been on our mind, but they were on His!

\*     \*     \*

When we looked at those Palestine miracles there was one important thing we didn't mention: the times when

Jesus our Lord immersed Himself in His heavenly Father. He "got away" for a little while, to return with God's love and power there for everyone to see . . . if they weren't too bigoted!

Perhaps we'll never realize how much it means to Him that we have managed a few minutes for God out of a crowded day. Yes, we're giving to Him, by making up a little for the millions who don't spare Him a thought. We're showing Him that we are in the minority which isn't frantically pursuing the world's dead-ends and illusions; we're making Him aware of our growing love and of our trust towards Him.

It is sometimes obviously quite a good idea, not even to mention the current problems, but just to relax in His love, knowing that, as we do so, He's working on those problems, anyway!

We are realizing, of course, that time spent with Jesus always saves time – time spent in abortive efforts, futile arguments, the nursing of hurt feelings, or hasty and compulsive "wrong moves".

Those who are greatly involved with people are always wise to realize how much those people are directly helped by the time spent alone with Jesus.

Our miracle-date can therefore be seen as a multiple receiving process: Jesus Himself receives during that time; we ourselves receive at great depth; many people whom we will now meet, or about whom we pray at such times, will receive.

There is great therapeutic value, by the way, in making some of those times apart with Jesus a chance quietly to adapt one or two of His own words found in the New Testament, bringing them into the first person.

He's giving me "the peace which the world cannot
    give" . . .
Thank You, Lord Jesus, for Your *peace*, now.

He's "making everything new" . . .
Thank You, Lord Jesus, that You're *renewing* me.

It is in times like this, also, that those promises which
Jesus made about life's difficulties can be allowed to
burn into us: "In this world you will have trouble . . .
but cheer up, I have conquered the world!"


## In Proportion


When we keep a date with Jesus, one of the things we
realize is His importance, compared with all the other
things which have been disturbing us. We begin to
realize that, because He is with us, we can lose our fear
of the threatening aspects. We can sense Jesus our Lord
coming between us and the disturbances from the world
around us, or those from within our own mental processes (we can't always tell the difference between these
two!)

At these times, we break off from watching the
world's confused working, and become aware of God's
very sure working – aware of things which He has
"completed" for us, or of things which He seems to be
working out for us. This recognition increases our
capacity to recognize God's opportunity-taking.

Our "miracle-dates" usually help us to be more
sharply aware, not only of God's identity, but of our
own. We stand back and see our life more as He sees it
– this can shock us occasionally, of course, but some
vital decisions and resolves at such times are quite

frequent! We are aware, too, of that crucial relationship being built up.

We have opened the doors . . . and not only has He come in to us, but we seem to have moved into a heavenly environment. We have opened the doors to a peace-experience for a little while. Having put Jesus at the centre of our thoughts, the miracle of peace can occur right in the middle of what could be a demanding or upsetting sort of day. By giving Jesus some of the attention which we might have continued giving to one or two other things, we've allowed Him to respond with a little miracle-activity.

We never come away from a "date" with Jesus quite the same as we were before, do we? The things that before that "date" we feel we should perhaps have put at the top of our list of activities, now turn out to be more efficiently dealt with.

Our brief period with the Lord has miraculously spilled over to help along the rest of the day. Times apart with Jesus are the high points of any day. They are quiet, but dynamic. They are vital contacts with the power which lies behind the creative process.

"Miracle-dates" turns out to be a true description, because of the greatly increased Divine opportunity-potential of such times.

Miracle-changes – not by tremendous efforts, or by complex "self-improvement" programmes, but just by being in contact!

Dear Lord,

You know about my commitments, but please show me lots of opportunities to keep a rendezvous with You – however short. Help me just to lay aside all the jarring things of my existence and, instead, to think about You.

In these times let me always be very conscious of Your love, Your wisdom, and Your power over all circumstances.

During these times with You, I know that You will be giving me a sense of proportion . . . the realization that, in Your love, there is absolutely nothing to fear.

Help me to remember that the occasions set apart for You are always opportunities for You to draw me closer to You.

I know this closeness will initiate deep and lasting miracle-changes in me, and help me to "share" You more excitingly with others.

Thank You

# 28

# Miracle-Partners

Miracle-partners. Well, there's a glib-sounding little title! I know that the title may sound rather pretentious – until you've actually experienced how God really does use you and me in His opportunity-taking.

If Jesus is involved in our still imperfect lives, and there's that growing awareness of His love, our contacts with people are wonderfully used. The partnership begins to have a much more exciting feel to it, of course, than our idea of "serving God". As far as the people we meet are concerned, we're not so much serving God as sharing Him.

Wonderfully used in the partnership, too, are our prayers!

\*     \*     \*

The placing of this chapter towards the end of our book does not mean that a great deal of miracle-work will have been necessary in us before we can be of use to others!

We may sometimes have a mental picture of a charismatic healing "personality", with authoritative voice, surrounded by the crutches and the discarded bottles of tablets, of those who have walked away from him, cured. Comparing ourselves with such a figure, we may feel that making a difference to other people's lives isn't exactly our vocation!

The truth is, of course, that God is sad when we look at our inadequacy, and feel that we could never be an agency for His miracles. It's staggering to look at some of those who have been very greatly used by God, to see how very inadequate and "unspiritual" they felt.

Like St Paul, God's miracle-partners are quite likely to have "something wrong" with them.

There is a man in England to whom many have come for healing prayer. He himself is afflicted with a very noticeable stammer. Among those who have received tremendous help from God through our friend with the stammer, are, in fact, one or two whose own stammering has been cured. But (you've guessed) – his own stammer remains! He just goes on being used by God.

Although things like speech-impediment, or another handicap, may remain in God's miracle-partners, there are usually miracle-changes of some kind in a person who puts himself or herself at God's disposal. This is because the influence *through* us, and the influence *in* us, are inseparable.


## *"Inadequate", But . . .*

The factor in being miracle-partners, of course, is not our self-confidence, or our feeling of spiritual "advancement", it's whether or not our life is genuinely centred on Jesus. If the Spirit of Jesus our Lord lives in us, that Spirit simply has to flow to those around us and there is, of course, such tremendous need in our world.

We must realize that feelings of inadequacy are so

often the starting point for miracles. Why? Well, of course, it's because our recognition of how little we amount to without Jesus, gives Him plenty of room in which to work! That is why Jesus our Lord achieves so much in our prayerful encounters with others, when we are probably very conscious of what we lack.

Our own natural hesitancy and inadequacy may well be detected by others, but He will be more readily seen.

The recognition today that God uses "wounded" healers is tremendously important. He finds great opportunities through people who feel very limited and vulnerable – but trust Him! His room to work is restricted when there is over-confidence, spiritual "posturing", a sense of status, or of professionalism. The self-emptying of Jesus our Lord must be our example here.

Another thing which restricts our Lord's work through us is if we are deliberately holding on to something in our life which, in our heart, we know is hurtful to Him. Jesus can use "weak" people in wonderful ways, but not those who have more than one Master.

Isn't it exciting that God not only allows us to work upon the raw material of our world, but lets us share what He's doing in people's lives? We are allowed to become part of that constant activity – rather like the dear old couple who had just bought a few shares in a huge international corporation, and said, "Have you seen that *we*'ve just opened a new factory in Nairobi?"

### The Caring Factor

There is something very important for us to notice here. Miracle-work is so often seen, essentially, as power.

We certainly saw the power of God wonderfully at

work through Jesus, but when we looked closely at those miracles earlier, we noticed, didn't we, how crucial was the presence of love? Jesus was not "trying out" God's power in Him, but loving people!

"My friend, *of course*, I want you to be well", to the leper.

"Now, stop being afraid", to the distracted Jairus.

Those eyes full of tenderness, and a very real sense of oneness with the sufferer. You might say that the healing process had already started, the moment Jesus looked with love upon a person's need.

If we feel that our "caring capacity" is not all that it might be, it's always a good idea to ask Jesus something like:

"Please, Lord, may Your love increase in me."

I'm sure that, at that moment, Jesus looks on us and says to Himself – "Now *there's* a child of Mine whom I can use." He will always respond to the request that His love should be in us, that we should see people as He does. And, of course, it will now be *His* love reaching people through us.

We see the effect of love, don't we, as little Peter comes in, bawling his head off after a bad tumble, or after being "wronged" in some way? Mum puts him on her knee, and instantly the power of her love is at work. It's not just a case of consoling words, but of an influence.

Very soon, Peter manages to force a smile – a little miracle of the sort which Mums can produce many times in a day. If Mums can produce that, need we ask what the infinite love of the risen Lord Jesus can bring about?

\*     \*     \*

The "flow" of love can be taken for granted when we're acting lovingly, even when tired or anxious, or when it's against our "inclination". His love will attract, and that's why it's worth ensuring that there is the steady aim of allowing that love to flow, whatever our present anxieties.

By the way, a little check-up on that "caring capacity" of ours can be repeated, from time to time, just in case (while busy with Christian causes) it has got a little rusty!

There will always be an influence, of course, from what we *are*, especially the love-element. So often we shall find that others have been uplifted by nothing in particular that we have said, but because of our presence – or rather, because of His in us!

What we venture to do as miracle-partners, if centred on Jesus, will not be recognized for its rather furious activity, but for its lasting effects. Things like peace, and a new sense of hope, will come, through us, into people's lives. Someone in contact with us will be drawn a little closer to Jesus our Lord.

If Jesus has touched someone's life through us, we can completely trust His greatness, that that person will be receiving precisely what is most needed.

\* \* \*

I remember, when I was a young journalist, listening to the late Dr Leslie Weatherhead. Near the end of his talk I forgot about taking notes, because I realized that he was saying something important for me.

"When you go outside," he said, "stand under the stars and tell God that in working out His purposes for this world He can count on you." Well, it so happened that it was a starry night, and I stood there and made that promise to God. I wasn't a very strong believer at that time, and I almost forgot the promise in the days which followed. But He remembered.

## At His Disposal

Miracle-partnership really begins from the moment that we ask Jesus our Lord to use us in the best way possible . . . *His* way. We soon find that He has been preparing one or two people for meeting us!

Some of these people may just be looking for a sympathetic ear (increasingly valued, these days, as a caring skill); some may want to talk about their lack of faith; some may ask us to pray for them (or *with* them, which becomes increasingly natural!) about a miracle they would like to see.

It's not essential, of course, but it's helpful, if we can keep some consciousness of Jesus's presence when we're with a person. That consciousness makes it absolutely certain that He's not going to waste the contact.

And those "Jesus-conscious" letters and 'phone calls won't be wasted either!

A consciousness of Jesus our Lord – if possible with a quiet pleasure in the thought of His love for us – is the ideal "base" for our reaching out to others.

## Change-Bringing

Sometimes the presence of Jesus may lead us to say an "unprepared" word of insight to someone. Often the reply will come, "Yes, that is exactly how I'm feeling.

How did you guess?" For a moment or two, Jesus had lifted our meeting with someone right out of the "ordinary" into another and very meaningful dimension. He had given us, in addition to the eye of love, the eye of truth.

On another occasion, we may find ourselves telling someone (very quietly, and without looking for any instant response) just what a difference Jesus can make, and how grateful we personally feel to Him. We find ourselves presenting Him, in fact, as the world's true hope. Nothing may happen at the time, but later, when meeting that person again, we are quite likely to be told that the previous encounter had started to change things a little! Jesus had used our encouraging or faith-building word, and begun one of those quiet miracles.

If we can keep close to our senior partner (very flexible about the "details" of the partnership), He is going to complete those well-intentioned, perhaps hesitant, things we feel led to do for Him.

And, if we're keeping close, many opportunities will be sent, rather than our having, rather feverishly, to "create" them.

\*     \*     \*

Two things worth mentioning concerning all Jesus's miracle-work through us are:

(a) quantity, and
(b) timing.

The lives of some of us are, of course, more restricted than others. We may be housebound, or almost permanently in hospital. Some of us may only see a handful of people in months. We should remember, therefore, that quantity is not the vital thing for God's partners. It is, of course, the quality of our contacts (or, if you like, the Jesus-factor) which really matters.

And even if we are in touch with many people, we must never go too far beyond our limits by forgetting to receive from Jesus, and to enjoy Him, as well as serving Him!

Timing is something we can't always be certain about. Certainly, prayer should precede action wherever possible (trusting our Lord to make us aware of that "urgent" person or situation). In very many cases, having given someone's needs in prayer to Jesus our Lord, we can be patient for a time, while He prepares the way for our eventual contact.

\* \* \*

We're absolutely safe, always, in thanking God that He "did something" with an encounter which we had. Through us, He may have pierced the darkness of a person's life; He may have begun, through us, a chain of events which will radically change someone's future; He may have started someone praying regularly for the first time.

All contacts which a miracle-partner has (however unpromising on the surface) are God's opportunities. Someone is being put in touch with His unique ability to make changes. It is as if a miracle-partner becomes a bridge between God and the needy person.

All those opportunities, with all sorts of people, occurring from that one little opportunity we originally gave to God!

One of the secrets of quiet joy is being able to give something of ourselves, in a natural way, both to our Lord Himself, and to some of His children.

We can look forward to many wonderful consequences of our meetings with people, as we begin to reflect some of Jesus's love.

By the way, it's so easy to "drop" a needy person whose "results" don't look very good on our record! We must *go on loving that person*, even if discouraged about an apparent lack of improvement or response.

When we feel that our love is being given without any real response, there is a vital thing to remember: at least one person is receiving – He told us that He did!

I'm sure that there's a wonderful law of love operating in this universe. If we are growing in harmony with that law (however imperfectly), then we can look forward to lasting achievements . . . as one of God's junior partners!

Dear Lord,

Thank You for calling those who are very aware of their weaknesses to share in Your work. I'm so glad that being used as Your miracle-partner does not depend on my perfection! I know that You are looking for my simple trust, and my putting of myself at Your disposal.

Lord, help me to recognize the opportunities which You send for me to express Your love. Help me to remember that You are in each one of those contacts.

Thank You for all that You are going to do through me.

Thank You that You will be making a difference in others' lives . . . whether I'm allowed to see that difference, or whether (patiently!) I just have to trust You.
Thank You

# 29

# Indispensable!

Remember that amazing bringing-back-to-life of Lazarus?

For a few moments outside that cave-tomb Jesus our Lord prayed. The prayer was not that His heavenly Father would sanction a miracle here (that was apparently dealt with a few days earlier). These seem to have been a few moments of realization. Jesus, the Divine Son, was experiencing the sense of complete harmony with God His Father. The power of God (even to give life to a man four days dead) could operate here, because Jesus was one with that power. Jesus was completely adjusted to God's activity. He was an extension of God.

As we watch Jesus call Lazarus back to life, we can begin to see the answer to the question so often asked: "What is the secret of answered prayer?" So many have been disappointed, when thinking that there is some sure "prayer technique", after which God will oblige.

The raising of Lazarus, and the other miracles, are the result of that wonderful state of harmony between Jesus and God the Father. None of us, of course, comes near to achieving that sense of one-ness! But we can see that if we're living a life which (in spite of imperfections) is Jesus-centred, then we are coming into harmony with a law which produces order out of chaos.

To take the opportunity of our prayer requests, our Lord is not looking for our technique, our intensity, or perhaps someone's dynamic image in front of a packed hall of expectant people. He's simply responding to a trusting relationship with Himself.

It is this relationship which is indispensable in answered prayers. You just can't sidestep Jesus's comparison about the vine-tree and the branches. "Live in Me . . . and I in you." Indispensable!

Prayer, for Jesus, was not a periodic activity, or a "department" of His life, it was a continuous state, just as His God-awareness was continuous.

Many people have found that prayer based on a relationship has enabled them to watch God bringing harmony into the most difficult circumstances; an experience which can be for each one of us.

\*       \*       \*

I didn't risk using the title "Miracle-Prayer" for this chapter because "Miracle-Prayer" might have seemed to stress, too much, the obtaining of miraculous answers through our prayer activity. In one or two places today, it is forgotten that true prayer doesn't always have miracles in mind!

I would, naturally, like us to look together at praying for others, as long as we don't forget that prayer is so much wider than this one "department".

Those quiet times thinking of Jesus's love, those trusting glances, those expressions of gratitude, those longings to be more like Him, are all part of that relationship-building – prayer, in fact, becoming more of our whole way of life. We have seen how just being "in contact", in all sorts of ways, makes a huge difference.

*In other words, prayer which isn't necessarily seeking a miracle can itself be miraculous.*

## Expectant, Not Impatient!

Having warned about our type of prayer not being too restricted, perhaps we might look now at noticing needs and praying expectantly. One of Jesus's miracle-partners certainly begins to detect needs in people!

This "awareness" is something which Jesus has been developing in us: the eye of love. And love is, as we have seen, the first principle of miracle-changes.

Noticing needs, by the way, does not mean an exaggerated and overpowering "Friend, you're in great need . . . You need what I've got" approach!

Our growing capacity for caring will just long for Jesus to help someone whose need we have noticed. This help may be our personal agency, or it may be, in very many cases, just through our love-based prayer.

The prayer of one of Jesus's miracle-partners is not followed by an impatient "demanding" of the answer, of course. The prayer is followed by a quiet expectancy . . . ready to see the answer when it shows up in someone's life, but, in any event, knowing that God is using the prayer.

\* \* \*

In hospital wards you can often see rather amazing things after a prayer has been said. You can see a patient's whole mood change. You can see that gaunt-looking character acquire optimism, sometimes becoming even more cheerful than you yourself may be feeling at that particular moment!

At times you can almost feel the peace which descends upon a person. It's not necessarily anything you *said* as a miracle-partner . . . much more likely to have been your invitation to Jesus to take this opportunity.

You can almost lose count of patients who show absolutely no change when prayed with, but who, on a second visit, say something like: "Do you know, after you left the other day? Well, I felt a little later as if there was a turning-point. I felt that things had begun to move in an upwards direction." Yes, an almost-formal little prayer said either at the bedside or later had, of course, brought in Jesus. He did the rest.

Sometimes people wonder why God uses human beings at all, when He's perfectly capable of performing miracles independently. In "limiting" Himself, to some extent, in order to depend on us, I am sure that one reason is that God enjoys the drawing closer to Himself which is involved in His using us. He enjoys our habit of prayer, which is becoming the basis for our whole life. He enjoys the closer relationship.

It's worth repeating that in all our contacts with people we must never lose that supernatural perspective. Every kind or practical thing we do, every encouragement we give, *must* be "surrounded" (perhaps later, when there's more time) by our prayer.

When our contacts with people are brief, we may never hear what difference our prayer for someone has made. Just occasionally if we've given our name and address to a friend we've just made, it is not unusual to hear later that God *did* take an opportunity in that encounter!

There's something very obvious which we may occasionally forget when actually praying for someone: *God's love for that person.*

We can for a few moments dwell on the fact that He *wants* to help that person, and is doing so . . . according to the present need, as *He* lovingly sees it. We must allow no doubts about our Lord's power to help, or about His use, in some way, of our prayer. We can be sure of His immediate influence in a situation. We need feel no tension . . . just a relaxing in what He is.

I must be careful not to suggest a "technique" (after all that we've said about miracle-producing techniques!), but I could mention that, when praying, I somehow try to "bring together" in my mind Jesus and the person prayed for. Many people pray this way – it's nothing original which I'm passing on!

Anyway, there, in the light of the Lord Jesus, we can begin to "see" what we trust will be the ultimate result of our prayer: the person in need, now happy, free from current imperfections and burdens, and drawn closer to Jesus. When praying, we can also claim God's victory on a person's behalf, and "see" that person disentangled from any complex or subtle holds which evil may have – there is usually something!

Remembering our look at those on-fire early disciples, we might keep in mind the desire for Jesus to show up well, rather than we ourselves, as the prayer is answered. Lots of thank-You's in anticipation of miracles are always appropriate, of course!

It should be remembered that, like creation itself, miracle-work is so often gradual. But when Jesus sees a need for rapid change, of course, He produces it.

*Bringing Together*

The offering to God of opportunities, by the way, is very effective in restoring relationships.

Results can be quite rapid. For example, when one of the parties during a blazing row leaves the room (always a good idea!) . . . then outside the room the present stormy relationship is "given" to Jesus . . . and the person returns to find, quite often, that the other party is now making friendlier noises.

Part of that brief prayer outside the room could have been "seeing" the two quarrellers together in the light of Jesus. I know that this could all sound like a bit of wish-fulfilment, or mere "coincidence" – if it wasn't for the fact that God proves the reality of His presence by so frequently changing an atmosphere of hostility.

If they're not given to Jesus, those situations can get dangerously worse, of course.

Obviously, the results of believing prayer of this sort are not always immediate. A "strained" situation may have to be endured a little longer (perhaps in order to face, and to put right, something whose continuance is harmful to the relationship). But the giving of the circumstances to Jesus has introduced a healing factor, which so often later shows itself as the emergence of love and understanding.

It's all part of spending even a second or two in handing over a situation to Jesus rather than over-reacting to it. How well repaid those few seconds usually are!

I know that it's almost a cliché to say that "no situation remains quite the same when you've prayed about it". I used to doubt whether this was always the case, but all that I have seen of Jesus our Lord's response to trusting prayer convinces me that it is true.

It is always dangerous to demand instant miracles, of course. But if our whole life is becoming more like an unbroken prayer, it is not usually too long before we see God, in some way, seizing the opportunity offered by one of His "inadequate" miracle-partners!

Dear Lord,

Thank You for using my prayers as opportunities for Your unique help to reach many people. Thank You that, as you see their need, You are at work in those lives.

I thank You, too, Lord Jesus, that You will use my prayers for people unknown to me in various parts of the world, where You see a need.

I think of them now . . .

Those who have lost someone greatly loved.
Those who see no point in living.
Those who live in constant fear.
Those who once knew love, but now feel that no one cares.
Those who are without the basic needs of food and shelter.
Those who are struggling to live with no knowledge of You.

Thank You, Lord, for linking people with Your resources, through my prayers.

Please increase Your love in me, so that the contacts of each day can be, increasingly, miracle-contacts.

Thank You

# 30

# Dark World . . .
# Bright Road

In talking about our expectation of miracles we may
seem to have been ignoring some harsh realities, and to
be in danger of becoming the "Cloud Seven" book
which we didn't want to be.

Watching God taking His opportunities, seeing
prayers answered, could still be seen by some as an
over-optimistic description of most people's experience
in following Jesus. Many others, of course, wouldn't
agree about the over-optimism!

Perhaps I should say again that expectation does not
mean false hopes. Life doesn't always respond to a
"miracles-or-nothing" attitude.

It would be naïve to say that, with Jesus involved, we
shall avoid pain, or doubt, or opposition. And there will
be conflicts not shared even by those closest to us.

But although the world can be so dark, the road
through it need not be. When Jesus our Lord said that
He would brighten up the road for us, it was no empty
phrase. The road, though illuminated by God's presence, has to be a narrow one. Much that is harmless
enough in itself, much that doesn't help that "closeness"
may have to be cheerfully relinquished, knowing that
He won't let there be a vacuum!

It's a road from which we shall wander frequently,

but one to which we shall always be so relieved to return.

Yes, it will often be a sad journey, but always one from which hope never disappears completely, as Jesus our Friend seems to lift us forward, even when we feel thoroughly disillusioned.

As we keep close to our Friend, the destination planned for us is that the love surrounding us here will one day be *seen*, in all its brightness and all its beauty.

\* \* \*

I feel that the realistic approach for each one of us is just to bank on Jesus taking lots of opportunities in our lives . . . but not to be discouraged when His miracle-work is temporarily undetected, or when things don't change in the way we would wish. We can be sure that Jesus is planning the best possible future for us – and all the time removing influences which would interfere with this.

A life involving Jesus always sees changes. With His perfect timing, our Lord is sure to be working on changes *now* which later we shall see as miraculous and decisive. And it won't always be a case of patiently hoping, of course. Some miracle-changes will quickly result from our developing relationship.

It will make such a difference, now, if we can see all life's events in relation to our future as God's children. Jesus our Lord has gone ahead of us to do a little preparatory work! This is no self-deception, but a logical consequence of the fact of God's existence, and of His burning interest in us.

We can never give Jesus our Friend too much of our attention, even if, occasionally, this attention earns for us the criticism about being "so heavenly-minded as to be of no earthly use"!

When we really let Jesus live, really give Him freedom in our lives, there is a reality about our relationship with Him. He starts to achieve His ambition for us to "lose" ourselves in Him. And we shall instinctively make Him our first resort, every time, in the challenge of new circumstances.

We shall recognize, I'm sure, that God's love for us, His miracle-work, and all that we try to do for Him, are one whole. If we are happy to be completely under His control, and open to His influence, those who know us will see miracle-changes in us, long before we do!

Immersing ourselves in Jesus's love, letting Him have a huge place in our lives, is going to be rewarded, I know, in so many ways. It may be the miracle we are looking for, or, even if that doesn't come to us, there will be miracles just as important, and there will be that unique sense of peace, that sense of "belonging".

Giving Jesus our love and our time is, of course, making up a little for a world which is still largely indifferent to Him.

## *Miracle-Forgetfulness!*

Many readers are perhaps not of the arms-raised-in-ecstasy kind when praising God. I'm not either, I'm afraid. I have realized, however, that indulging in a little worship of Jesus – whether extrovert or quiet – is increasingly enjoyable . . .

Thanking and praising our Lord for Himself is something we can do in most surroundings, and we find ourselves progressing, gradually, almost to a *state* of worship, as far as Jesus is concerned, worship which doesn't necessarily have one eye on the next possible miracle!

When circumstances are extremely difficult, a few minutes of praise – for which the initial effort may be hard – is the very best thing we can be doing at the moment.

With perhaps little warmth of feeling, we nevertheless press on with the expression of trust and gratitude which He knows is good for us. The Lord knows that we, as well as He Himself, are receiving at such times, though we may not realize it immediately. As we said earlier, our mind may not be on miracles at that moment – but nevertheless it's very likely that they are quietly happening!

*     *     *

Although it's true that love is the one thing which endures, there will be many reading this who, sadly, have never found a close and satisfying human love.

But it's as if God is poised ready to take what, for Him, is a very special opportunity, where there is someone with an "unfulfilled" existence. He wants us to be aware of the one completely satisfying and permanent love. This love guarantees that, one day, every deep longing not fulfilled here, will be wonderfully realized.

The love of Jesus is an influence which wears down so much that is negative, and our experience of it, of course, brings great joy to Him. It's wonderful to experience (rather than just assent to) the fact that every detail of our life *is* important to God. His activity in those details is just a tiny foretaste of what He is saving up for us. He will not only bring harmony out of the details, but *use* them on our journey towards that perfection which just now seems so remote.

God's plans *must* be accomplished – that's why He is deeply involved, and active. The promise of Jesus our Lord is, as we know, that one day we shall be with Him in the place where love is everything. That is a promise which, because of His greatness, He is able to keep.

When we reach that place, there will be nothing else to wish for. His love will be all that we shall need. There will be no more miracle-changes to watch out for!

What would be a reasonable forecast for the remainder of our life, assuming that we are trying to keep close to Jesus, and learning to recognize His opportunity-taking?

It's as if the realism of Jesus our Lord is saying to us, in our very varied personal circumstances: "You will experience much darkness in the material world, but I will illuminate so many places for you. I will give you many glimpses of the real existence . . . the world of the Spirit, which will eventually be your environment. Until that day, the process of drawing back My world to Myself is one which you can share in, and enjoy. At every moment you are completely safe in My love."

\*   \*   \*

There is surely no greater thing we can do with our life than to let it be, as far as we possibly can, one *huge* opportunity for God . . .

I am sure that what is needed now, at the end of this book, is not some well-polished concluding sentence by me.

Let our very deeply-involved Lord Jesus have the final word. He says:

## God's Opportunities

Do not let your heart be troubled . . .

I am always with you . . .

Live within My love . . .

All power in heaven and on earth is Mine . . .

Ask, and you will receive . . . and your joy will be
complete!

\*    \*    \*

# Also available in Fount Paperbacks

## *Journey for a Soul*
### GEORGE APPLETON

'Wherever you turn in this inexpensive but extraordinarily valuable paperback you will benefit from sharing this man's pilgrimage of the soul.'

*Methodist Recorder*

## *The Imitation of Christ*
### THOMAS A KEMPIS

After the Bible, this is perhaps the most widely read book in the world. It describes the way of the follower of Christ – an intensely practical book, which faces the temptations and difficulties of daily life, but also describes the joys and helps which are found on the way.

## *Autobiography of a Saint: Thérèse of Lisieux*
### RONALD KNOX

'Ronald Knox has bequeathed us a wholly lucid, natural and enchanting version . . . the actual process of translating seems to have vanished, and a miracle wrought, as though St Teresa were speaking to us in English . . . his triumphant gift to posterity.'

*G. B. Stern, The Sunday Times*

## *The Way of a Disciple*
### GEORGE APPLETON

'. . . a lovely book and an immensely rewarding one . . . his prayers have proved of help to many.'

*Donald Coggan*

# Also available in Fount Paperbacks

BOOKS BY C. S. LEWIS

## The Abolition of Man

'It is the most perfectly reasoned defence of Natural Law (Morality) I have ever seen, or believe to exist.'

*Walter Hooper*

## Mere Christianity

'He has a quite unique power for making theology an attractive, exciting and fascinating quest.'

*Times Literary Supplement*

## God in the Dock

'This little book . . . consists of some brilliant pieces . . . This is just the kind of book to place into the hands of an intellectual doubter . . . It has been an unalloyed pleasure to read.'

*Marcus Beverley, Christian Herald*

## The Great Divorce

'Mr Lewis has a rare talent for expressing spiritual truth in fresh and striking imagery and with uncanny acumen . . . it contains many flashes of deep insight and exposures of popular fallacies.'

*Church Times*

# Also available in Fount Paperbacks

## A Gift for God
### MOTHER TERESA OF CALCUTTA

'The force of her words is very great . . . the message is always the same, yet always fresh and striking.'

*Malcolm Muggeridge*

## Strength to Love
### MARTIN LUTHER KING

'The sermons . . . read easily and reveal a man of great purpose, humility and wisdom . . . in the turbulent context of the American race conflict, Dr King's statements have the ring of social as well as spiritual truth . . .'

*Steven Kroll*
*The Listener*

## A Book of Comfort
### ELIZABETH GOUDGE

'The contents are worth ten of the title: this is a careful, sensitive anthology of the illuminations in prose and verse that have prevented the world from going wholly dark over the centuries.'

*Sunday Times*

## The Desert in the City
### CARLO CARRETTO

'. . . we have been in the hands of one of the finest of modern spiritual writers, who helps us on the road of love in Christ.'

*Philip Cauvin, the Universe*

# Fount Paperbacks

Fount is one of the leading paperback publishers of religious books and below are some of its recent titles.

- [ ] THE WAY OF THE CROSS Richard Holloway £1.95
- [ ] LIKE WIND ON THE GRASSES Rita Snowden £1.95
- [ ] AN INTRODUCTION TO MARITAL PROBLEMS Jack Dominian £2.50
- [ ] I AM WITH YOU John Woolley £2.95
- [ ] NOW AND FOR EVER Anne Townsend £1.95
- [ ] THE PERFECTION OF LOVE Tony Castle £2.95
- [ ] A PROPHETIC PEOPLE Clifford Hill £2.95
- [ ] THOMAS MORE Richard Marius £7.95
- [ ] WALKING IN THE LIGHT David Winter £1.95
- [ ] HALF WAY Jim Thompson £2.50
- [ ] THE HEART OF THE BIBLE George Appleton £4.95
- [ ] I BELIEVE Trevor Huddleston £1.75
- [ ] PRESENT CONCERNS C. S. Lewis £1.95
- [ ] PSALMS OF PRAISE Frances Hogan £2.50
- [ ] MOTHER TERESA: CONTEMPLATIVE IN THE HEART OF THE WORLD Angelo Devananda £2.50
- [ ] IN THE HURRICANE Adrian Hastings £2.50

All Fount paperbacks are available at your bookshop or newsagent, or they can be ordered by post from Fount Paperbacks, Cash Sales Department, G.P.O. Box 29, Douglas, Isle of Man, British Isles. Please send purchase price plus 15p per book, maximum postage £3. Customers outside the UK send purchase price, plus 15p per book. Cheque, postal order or money order. No currency.

NAME (Block letters)_____

ADDRESS_____

_____